ARTEMIS CHILD

a rain of stars

ARTEMIS CHILD

a rain of stars

Diane Ioannou

ISBN: 979-8-9868875-3-1
E-ISBN: 979-8-9868875-4-8

Cover and interior design by Tabitha Lahr
Front cover photo by Tyler Locket

Printed in the United States of America

*"All endings are also beginnings.
We just don't know it at the time."*
—MITCH ALBOM, *The Five People
You Meet in Heaven*

In memory of my beloved godmother Voula
Though I thought that I would see you
one more time again . . .

When you wish upon a star
Makes no difference who you are
Anything your heart desires
Will come to you.

If your heart is in your dreams
No request is too extreme
When you wish upon a star
As dreamers do.

Fate is kind
She brings to those who love
The sweet fulfillment of
Their secret longing

Like a bolt out of the blue
Fate steps in and sees you through
When you wish upon a star
Your dreams come true

When stars are born
They possess a gift or two
One of them is this . . .

They have the power to make a wish come true.

BY LEIGH HARLINE AND
NED WASHINGTON

PROLOGUE

The Legendary Perseus

Many years ago, there was a beautiful princess named Danae who lived in the city of Argos of a country named Greece. She was the daughter of King Acrisius, although she was not his wife Queen Eurydice's biological child. Instead, Danae was the result of an extramarital affair and was given to the Queen to raise by her true mother, the naiad Aganippe.

Aganippe resided in the Mount Helicon region of Boeotia. An area assigned to her by her father, the river god Permessus, to protect. She lived near a magical spring at the base of the mountain named after her—the Aganippe Spring.

The Nine Muses, also known as the Aganippides, lived in a grove next to the spring and frequently visited it to perform enchantments.

From the spring gushed "sweet waters of inspiration" of poetry, music, and the arts.

And those who visited the spring to bathe and drink from it found themselves speaking in rhymes.

The birth and life of Perseus was no ordinary story for he was no ordinary human being.

King Acrisius was fraught with distraught for he was unable to father a son to succeed him on the throne. In his despair, he journeyed to Delphi to consult with the oracle on what to do.

The oracle's reply was: "Not only will you not attain a son, but you are also destined to be killed by your own grandson."

It was all she said. No explanations given. No recommendations made.

Interpreting the prophecy to mean that Danae's unborn son would bring about his demise, the king was greatly troubled. He knew that harming Danae would incur the wrath of Aganippe, whose name meant "the mare who kills mercifully."

He called in his top advisors, to consult with them on what to do, but they were of no help.

After giving it a lot of thought, the king came up with an idea. He commanded the construction of a magnificent tower in the palace courtyard to house the young princess.

The tower was designed to fill all the princess's needs, but there was a catch. The tower lacked doors and windows, with only one opening at the rooftop. An opening to the sky.

It was an effort to prevent the unpreventable. Or at least, buy some time.

Aganippe was infuriated upon learning that her daughter had been imprisoned in a tower. She immediately sought out the god Zeus and begged for his assistance. Zeus agreed to help.

The princess was crying herself to sleep, as she did every night, when she suddenly felt something strange. She opened her eyes to see that the sky was not dark as usual; instead, it was filled with golden stars. As she admired them, the stars transformed into a shower of gold that streamed through the sky opening.

It was Zeus himself. He came to Danae in the form of golden rain and impregnated her without her knowledge.

It was the moment Perseus was divinely conceived—"under a rain of stars."

What was King Acrisius to do? For in addition to the wrath of Aganippe, he now had to worry about the wrath of Perseus's father, Zeus.

King Acrisius was in a difficult situation. He knew that to harm either mother or child meant that he would face punishment worse than death.

As a result, he commanded that Danae and her baby be taken out of the tower and placed in a chest made of wood, which would be thrown into the sea.

Yes, Danae, along with her newborn son were freed from the tower, but they were now facing the challenge of strong waves carrying them far from the shores and into the deep waters.

Upon hearing Danae's fearful prayers Zeus called upon Poseidon to protect them until they reached their final destination—the island of Seriphos.

Poseidon responded by calming the seas and guiding them safely to shore.

Early in the morning, as the sun was rising, Dictis was on his way to his boat for fishing when he stumbled upon a wooden chest by the water's edge. To his surprise, he found a sleeping mother and her infant inside.

Without hesitation he picked them up and brought them to his home. Once there, he covered them with warm blankets and offered Danae some water to drink. He then prepared a meal for her to eat.

Dictis lived alone in a humble abode near the shore where Danae and baby Perseus had washed up. He was a gentle, compassionate, and respectful man who welcomed them into his home.

Over the years, Dictis provided them with a safe and comfortable sanctuary. He not only took good care of them but also raised Perseus as though he was his own son.

Not long after hearing about the rescue, Dictis' brother, Polydectes, paid them a visit. As soon as he laid eyes on Danae, he was instantly captivated by her beauty.

Polydectes, who ruled over Seriphos, became envious. "How is it possible a mere fisherman has such a beautiful princess living with him."

He repeatedly offered Danae a place in his grand mansion, promising her and her son everything they could possibly desire and the best care from his servants.

However, Danae turned down all Polydectes' proposals.

As he was growing up, Perseus wanted nothing to do with Polydectes because he believed him to be of bad character and did not trust him. Perseus became protective of his mother as he got older, always ensuring she stayed away from Polydectes.

Polydectes had tried time and time again to befriend the young Perseus, but to no avail.

Eventually Polydectes gave up and began thinking of ways to get rid of him.

He confided in a trusted companion, "making Perseus leave Seriphos and never return was the only solution."

Polydectes devised what he believed was "a foolproof plan" to eliminate Perseus once and for all.

He called upon the inhabitants of Seriphos for an important announcement. "I have decided to marry Princess Hippodamia, daughter of King Oenomaus of Pisa," he declared.

Perseus was overjoyed at the news, oblivious to the horrors that had befallen Hippodamia's previous suitors.

Polydectes hosted a banquet in his courtyard and invited all the islanders.

After the feast, he asked for their help in achieving his goal and promised to remember their assistance. "Once I become the wealthy king of Pisa, I promise to take care of all your needs."

"I need gifts to win the hand of Princess Hippodamia, and as she loves horses, I ask that each of you bring me a horse."

Perseus was thrilled at the idea of Polydectes departing the island. He envisioned Dictis assuming the role of ruler over Seriphos. With Dictis harboring feelings for his mother, the two could unite in marriage and govern the island jointly.

This outcome would be ideal for Perseus; he could embark on journeys and adventures, unburdened by concerns for his mother's welfare.

There was only one problem, Perseus had no horse to offer. So instead, Perseus quickly came up with an alternative offer: "Tell me any gift you desire, and I assure you that I won't decline it."

Polydectes was pleased to hear that. And Perseus had openly declared it in front of all the guests as witnesses.

Polydectes smiled as he called out in response: "I want the severed head of Medusa!"

Bringing back the severed head of Medusa was no easy task. This Perseus knew. He had heard stories about the gorgon monster and previous attempts to kill her. And that Medusa had the power to turn brave men into stone with just one glance at her face.

Polydectes had forced him to keep his foolish promise. He insisted that Perseus should not waste any time and set sail for the task.

Realizing he required divine assistance, Perseus called upon the goddess of wisdom. Athena materialized and consented to assist him in commencing the task. Furthermore, she assured him that she would be available until its completion. All he had to do was call upon her.

Perseus found great comfort in Athena's assurances and following her instructions he set sail to begin his journey.

He first sailed south to the shores of North Africa in search of the Hesperides, the nymphs of the evening.

The Hesperides resided in a blissful garden near the Atlas Mountains. Athena explained that they were in possession of an important item that Perseus needed right after defeating the Gorgon.

The Hesperides appeared skeptical until Perseus explained that the goddess Athena sent him. This seemed to clarify everything.

They handed him a knapsack.

As he continued his journey Perseus received a visit from his father Zeus, who bestowed upon him an Adamantine sword and wished him courage and victory.

This sword was not ordinary; it was made of the highest tier of Hardmode and was said to be indestructible.

Additionally, the sword had a sickle protrusion near the tip, which would be useful for beheading Medusa.

Perseus also received a visit from Zeus's brother, the god of darkness. Hades gifted Perseus with the helm of darkness, an invisible cloak that he could throw over himself to escape unnoticed.

Hermes also paid Perseus a visit and gave him a pair of winged sandals. Hermes instructed Perseus to use the sandals to fly away, if necessary, but he would have to return them after completing his task.

While Perseus was admiring the sandals, Athena appeared with a polished bronze shield. The shield was *so bright that he was momentarily blinded by its reflection. Athena handed the shield to him, saying "This will come in very handy." Perseus examined the shield before looking up to speak with Athena, but she had already disappeared.*

Equipped with all the necessary gifts, Perseus proceeded to sail north to the island of Sarpedon. (An ancient island where Medusa lived and roamed which was located near the island of Lesbos).

Upon reaching its shores Perseus armed himself with all the gifts and began his quest to locate the Gorgon's home—a cave situated somewhere above the shores.

The cave was not hard to find as there were over a hundred stone statues standing outside its entrance. A warning to anyone who dared to venture inside.

Many were once great leaders and warriors who were sent there from nearby kingdoms. By kings who were all terrified by the same thought—that the powerful gorgon monster would one day escape the island and make her way to their lands.

Perseus found the cave entrance but did not proceed. Instead, he hid behind some nearby bushes and waited until nightfall.

When nightfall came and it was completely dark, Perseus picked up all his gifts and proceeded to the cave entrance.

After taking a deep breath he entered the cave.

It did not take long to locate Medusa. He walked a couple of steps past the entrance and saw her. She was laying on a raised surface deep inside the cave sound asleep.

Perseus took another deep breath. Then slowly he walked toward the raised surface.

Once he felt he was close enough, he quietly turned himself around as he gently lifted the reflective bronze shield with his left hand.

In his right hand he was holding his Adamantine sword.

Using the shield as a mirror, he located the sleeping gorgon's reflection on it.

Then he adjusted the shield to have a clear view of the sleeping gorgon's head. He continued to cautiously walk (still backwards) toward her.

It had not taken long for Perseus to figure out what Athena had meant about the polished shield "coming in handy."

He realized that if Medusa awoke, by looking at her reflection he had a good chance of leaving the cave. For her reflection would not turn him into stone.

Medusa was still sound asleep. Perseus continued to get closer. Once he felt that he was close enough, he lifted his Adamantine sword.

After taking a third deep breath he quickly swung the Adamantine sword.

Perseus had hit his target!

Yes, Perseus succeeded. He managed to cut off the gorgon monster's head with one well-calculated precise swing.

Medusa heard the swift sword swing and opened her eyes in alarm, but it was too late. Despite seeing the sword approaching her, she only had time to let out a piercing scream.

Looking away, Perseus reached down to pick up the severed snake-covered head, which had rolled from the raised surface to the ground. He could feel the snakes still moving as he cautiously inserted it into the knapsack.

He was just about to walk away when he noticed movement in Medusa's headless body.

As he looked over, he saw two beings springing out of her severed neck.

It seemed Medusa was unknowingly pregnant when Athena transformed her into a gorgon monster. And, as a result of her beheading, her two unborn children who had been trapped inside her were now free.

They were Pegasus (an immortal winged horse), and Chysaor (a golden-sworded boy) who stood before Perseus gazing at him.

Stheno and Euryale, Medusa's two immortal gorgon sisters, heard her horrible piercing scream. But by the time they got to the cave, it was too late. All they found was Medusa's son, Chysaor, standing over and staring at his mother's lifeless headless body.

It did not take long to figure out that Perseus was responsible for their sister's death, for they found his sailboat docked on the nearby shore.

Believing he would need to return to the boat to leave the island, they waited for him to appear.

When he failed to show up, the Gorgons concluded that he must be hiding somewhere on the island. However, despite their thorough search of the entire area, they were unable to find any trace of him.

Accompanied by his new friend, the white winged Pegasus, Perseus managed to escape from the cave and the entire island, using the helm of darkness to remain unnoticed and invisible.

Perseus was amazed at Pegasus's speed and maneuverability, which enabled them to travel quickly and evade detection.

By the time Medusa's sisters began to search the island, they were already far away.

Chysaor, who wielded a golden sword, remained on the island. He was brought up by Medusa's monster sisters and eventually wedded the naiad Callirhoe. Together they had two monstrous offspring: Geryon, a terrifying giant with three heads, and Echidna, a creature that was half-woman and half-snake.

Perseus, accompanied by his immortal friend Pegasus, decided to explore new places and make new acquaintances before heading back to Seriphos.

Their journey began on the nearby shores of Anatolia, where Perseus was highly praised for his accomplishments.

Perseus had achieved his ultimate goal of traveling and experiencing new adventures. Moreover, he gained the attention of wealthy and powerful leaders who were eager to meet with him.

Many kings invited him to their kingdoms and showered him with lavish gifts. He had stayed with them and become acquainted with their families. This had earned him widespread recognition as a renowned hero in the whole of the eastern Mediterranean region.

As the son of princess Danae, Perseus was aware that he was the rightful heir to the throne of the kingdom of Argos, and he planned to assert his claim to the position soon.

With all the recognition he had earned, he was now poised to become a formidable and well-connected king.

As their journey neared its end, Perseus and Pegasus began their return trip to Seriphos.

However, an unusual occurrence interrupted their travels.

While passing over a coastal town situated on the edge of the Nile River, south of the Sahara, Perseus observed some peculiar activity in the water below.

He steered Pegasus down to investigate.

As they got closer, he could not believe his eyes. A young naked maiden stood chained hands and feet to a large boulder protruding from the water.

She was in great distress desperately trying to free herself by moving her arms and legs while crying out for help.

As he turned his head, Perseus quickly realized the reason why.

A massive sea serpent was making its way through the river and heading straight for the chained maiden.

Perseus instructed Pegasus to dive while reaching for his sword.

He began taunting the creature with insults, diverting its attention from the vulnerable chained up maiden.

The agitated serpent stopped in its tracks before turning its focus to chase after Perseus and Pegasus.

Perseus instructed Pegasus to fly at a low altitude and make various maneuvers to avoid the sea serpent's pursuit.

Eventually, the monster grew weary and paused to catch its breath.

This was the opportune moment that Perseus had been waiting for. He directed Pegasus straight towards the serpent, and bravely engaged in battle with it.

It was a long and arduous battle with Perseus ultimately defeating the serpent.

After confirming the sea serpent was dead, Perseus guided Pegasus toward the boulder.

Upon landing, he dismounted and went over to release the chained maiden.

She was still trembling with fear but very grateful to be free.

Perseus kindly draped his cape over her shivering body and held her close to soothe her. In that moment, he was captivated by her radiance and physical allure.

They both stood in wordless awe. She, grateful for the safety he provided and he in admiration of her beauty which seemed to rival that of the goddess Aphrodite.

He gently lifted her onto Pegasus and positioned himself in front of her, instructing her to hold on tight.

With a shout, Pegasus soared into the sky, carrying them to the nearest town.

Upon arriving in the town, Perseus discovered that she was no ordinary maiden. She was princess Andromeda, the daughter of the wealthy King Cepheus, ruler of Aethiopia.

After the townspeople dressed her properly the two of them rode Pegasus to the nearby palace.

There, Perseus approached the king and claimed the beautiful Andromeda to be his in marriage, believing he earned it by saving the princess from the sea monster.

The king was happy to oblige, having heard of Perseus's heroic deed of slaying Medusa. Perseus and Andromeda were given their own section of the royal palace to live in, but Perseus made it clear that he would eventually have to return to Seriphos.

So, why was Princess Andromeda stripped of all her clothing and tied to a large boulder in the Nile River?

The tale starts with Queen Cassiopeia bragging about her daughter's beauty, which she claimed was equal to that of the Nile Naiads.

The boasting caught the attention of Poseidon, the god of the Naiads, who was not at all pleased with the Queen's behavior.

In response, Poseidon sent massive waves into the Nile, causing flooding in Aethiopia. To make matters worse, Poseidon also unleashed the Sea Serpent Cetus to destroy all living creatures.

King Cepheus sought advice from the oracle of Ammon on how to rid his kingdom of the terrifying sea monster that was causing destruction.

The oracle's response was "No relief would be found until you expose your daughter Andromeda to the sea monster."

"What about the princess' fate?" the concerned king added.

"She will either be taken or killed by the sea serpent," was the reply.

So, it was with a heavy heart and to save the land and his people that the king had ordered this action.

After their royal wedding, Perseus and Andromeda moved into the palace, where they lived happily with the king and queen.

Soon after, they welcomed their first child, a son they named Perses.

However, shortly after, Perseus began to feel homesick and restless.

By now he had heard the stories about King Oenomaus of Pisa. That he was in fear of a prophecy that "he would be killed by a son-in-law." And that every suitor who had sought Hippodamia's hand in marriage so far had met their demise in a deadly chariot race.

It was then that Perseus realized that he had been sent away by Polydectes so that he could pursue his mother. He knew Polydectes was no hero and would never compete in such a perilous contest.

After discussing it, Perseus and Andromeda decided to embark on the journey together. They planned to first visit Seriphos to straighten matters out before heading to Argos, where Perseus would assert his right to his grandfather's throne.

Since he had no sons, King Cepheus requested Perseus and Andromeda to leave behind the young Prince Perses.

The king assured them that Perses would receive excellent education and training to become a great ruler in the future.

Perseus and Andromeda had agreed. They started preparing for their journey.

King Cepheus generously provided them with a large ship filled with precious gifts, along with soldiers and servants for their protection and care.

As predicted by the king, Prince Perses grew up to be a great ruler and powerful king. He not only ruled over Aethopia, but also conquered and ruled other lands, establishing his own grand dynasty.

King Perses would eventually become such a revered and legendary king that the country of Persia and its people, the Persians, were named in his honor.

Upon returning to Seriphos, Perseus discovered that his mother was in hiding due to Polydectes' aggressive behavior.

Perseus immediately went over to confront Polydectes. He brought his knapsack along.

Polydectes was taken aback by Perseus's sudden appearance, as he didn't think Perseus could have completed the seemingly impossible task.

As Perseus entered the courtyard, he saw Polydectes sitting on a raised, intricately carved armchair. This was the spot where he received his guests.

"How about the fulfillment of your promise?" Polydectes firmly asked.

Perseus stood before him, ready to respond.

"See for yourself," a smiling Perseus responded as he reached into the knapsack and pulled out Medusa's severed head.

Polydectes met his end through this act, as the sight of Medusa's face caused him to transform into stone.

It seemed that even though severed, Medusa's head retained its ability to turn people into stone.

The eyes still had a powerful glow, and those who stood in front of it could not help but look upon them.

It became an additional powerful weapon for Perseus' arsenal. A dangerously powerful one.

With Polydectes out of the picture the joyful Dicits proposed to Danae whom he had loved and cared for all along.

The couple moved into Polydectes' former mansion, which now boasted a new piece of art in its courtyard—a stone statue of the former ruler.

Dictis and Danae became the esteemed "King and Queen" of the now prosperous island of Seriphos, for Perseus and Andromeda bestowed them with many magnificent gifts.

The prophecy of the Delphic oracle regarding the death of Perseus's grandfather was also soon fulfilled.

The most popular version of the story was told by Pausanias. According to this version, Perseus was in Larissa to participate in various athletic games. He was also there to introduce a new competitive sport that he had invented called "The Quoit."

The game involved throwing a ring of iron to encircle or land as close as possible to an upright peg.

According to the story, Perseus was demonstrating the sport to a crowd when his exiled grandfather happened to step into its trajectory.

King Acrisius was immediately killed.

Following his grandfather's death, Perseus was offered the kingdom of Argos but refused it out of shame for having caused his grandfather's demise.

Instead, he traded it for the kingdom of Tiryns. However, Perseus did not remain king of Tiryns for very long, he quickly began construction of the citadel of Mycenae, establishing his own kingdom.

Perseus and Andromeda found happiness ruling the kingdom of Mycenae with their eight additional children.

Perseus got to keep all his gifts, except for Hermes' winged sandals which he returned after accomplishing his task.

He had not needed them for he had his loyal winged horse Pegasus to fly around with.

Together, they continued to travel, often unseen in the darkness.

However, their journeys became less frequent and shorter for Perseus now had important responsibilities—a kingdom to rule and a family to take care of.

CHAPTER 1

It happened during the fall. Maria was away, in Southern California, for a couple of months to spend time with her children and visit loved ones and friends.

Some said that the workers of the house being built nearby hit it with their tractor. Others claimed a truck ran into it in the early morning hours and quickly backed up and left the scene. Yet others insisted none of that happened. That it came down all by itself due to heavy rains.

Regardless, once Maria got back, she found large stones and dirt of what used to be the village oven ruins on the pathway below.

The neighbors were fuming mad, yelling, and accusing her of deliberately causing the collapse.

She had promptly contacted her contractor and insisted that he contact the appropriate town office to resolve the issue and to have it all cleared up.

Maria did her best to be a considerate neighbor and solve the problem. She went as far as proposing to park her car on the street so that her neighbors could use her allocated parking space. However, nothing seemed to please them.

By now Maria realized that things were not always
what they seemed, at least not in these parts of Greece.
The local saying and belief of "what is yours is ours" had
played a role in this episode of "the village oven drama,"
and there would be more episodes to follow.

The contractor called and within a week the town
office dispatched a bulldozer and a pickup truck to clean
up the area.

Maria was sitting working at her desk while the bulldozer cleared out the rubble. At the same time, she kept
an eye on the cleanup by looking up every so often.

She noticed that the affected neighbors had walked
over and were now chatting with the workers.

Her experience in the small port town taught her
always to expect the unexpected, so she kept a vigilant
eye on them.

Sure enough, the unexpected would soon happen.

Most of the work had been completed with very
little remaining to clean up when the official in charge
departed from the scene.

And that's when it happened!

The tractor collided with the remaining corner of the
oven ruins dislodging the rectangular cut stones that held
the lower-level dirt in place. As a result, the dirt was once
again falling onto the pathway below.

The tractor operator did not act alone. Maria noticed
the neighbor whispering something into his ear, instructing
him to cut the corner.

Maria saw it happen but there was not anything she
could do to stop it, for it occurred abruptly.

The damage was irreversible. The only thing she could do was to find her camera and take pictures to use as evidence, which she did almost immediately.

Then she went down to ask the tactor operator for an explanation.

"Why did you do that?" Maria asked him with an angry tone.

"It's just a small bit on the corner, no big deal" the neighbor responded instead.

Maria ignored him. He was the same neighbor who previously complained about the rocks and dirt obstructing his walkway. And now, as a result of this latest action, more rocks and dirt would fall!

The tractor operator did not speak a word.

"I've paid for the parcel where the village oven stood," Maria exclaimed. "You had no authority to encroach and cut into my land!"

Maria was certain that the parcel corner was not cut accidentally. And she suspected that each, both the neighbor and the operator, had their own motives for doing so.

Her neighbor wanted the soil on the parcel of land to be leveled so that Maria couldn't build her sundeck or anything else on it. He wanted it to be used as a neighborhood parking lot instead.

And he would have succeeded.

If she hadn't acted, the soil would have eroded due to the heavy winter rains. And because of the strict building restrictions, Maria wouldn't be able to build anything on the parcel again.

The bulldozer operator didn't care about the other details. He was focused on the rectangular cornerstones for the large stones were hand-chiseled, costly, and rare.

THE ORDEAL REMINDED MARIA of a political satire saying which dated back to the 1960s. The saying went, "Τα δικά μας δικά μας και τα δικά σας ξανά δικά μας," which translated to "What's ours is ours, and what's yours is again ours!"

Maria then recalled an article she had read on social media about the nearby town of Argos and its cultural history. It had included a section on how residents viewed foreigners in the 1960s.

The article defined a foreigner as "anyone who wasn't a local." This meant that someone from a different part of Greece or someone born in the area returning to their roots were also considered foreigners.

The locals would ask, "Why are you here and what are you trying to get from us?" If the foreigner seemed vulnerable or naive, the locals perceived them as weak and their next thought was "Since you're not trying to get something from us, let's see what we can get from you!"

YES, HER EXPERIENCE WAS ANOTHER instance of an outdated culture that was still prevalent in the Peloponnese.

Maria immediately called the town office to report what had happened. She also obtained an email address and sent pictures of the cut corner.

She explained how she would have to pay extra to have the corner rebuilt and that some stones had fallen into the adjacent patio, damaging her furniture. (She discovered this when she went to talk to the tractor operator).

Maria then spoke to her contractor demanding he follow up with the town office to get permission and build the corner and cement the top.

The dirt continued to fall out of the cut corner. Days went by, then weeks went by, and nobody was doing anything.

She then called the office official one last time. "If things don't get corrected, I will get an attorney!" She was not going to wait for the parcel to get washed away.

Maria was neither naive nor vulnerable. She knew that if she took legal action, she would win the case. That even if she did not go to court a call from the attorney would get the project moving again.

It worked. Soon the contractor was given the go-ahead. The workers came to build up the corner and also cement the top of the parcel. Per Maria's request, they also put stucco on the sides.

Now the sundeck was starting to take shape.

What a test of patience. It was a virtue Maria lacked an abundance of.

Maria had found the locals all knew each other. Often, they were related to one another. Because of this, there were all sorts of ways of interfering with others' affairs.

The concept of healthy boundaries did not exist in their daily life, for their daily routines consisted of fighting off competition and "enemies."

An enemy was someone who did not follow the unspoken rules of allowed behavior. In not doing so you became a victim of made-up stories and gossip. If that did not stop you, as Maria would later learn, there were other means to make you behave.

Maria's sundeck project kept getting stuck from the very beginning. Even though she had written permission from both the historical and archeological departments to bring down the large stones, she had faced opposition.

The building department told the contractor that he also needed to get the go-ahead from them. With no reason or details given. It seemed that local government employees would purposely freeze projects, then ask for money to get them moving again.

Due to the Coronavirus pandemic, all that would soon change.

The Greek government moved quickly to put in place new programs and policies. They got as many services as they could online. This way the residents of Greece would not run the risk of infection.

That meant that Maria's contractor and engineer could now file for permits on an online government site. And they did!

It was as though the government had a backup plan for a possible pandemic or other nationwide catastrophe. For the change happened almost immediately.

Maria recalled waiting in a long line at the bank where there was only one bank teller available. The customer in front of her complained "why is there only one line?" The response was "the bank wants its customers to get online and stop coming into the bank."

It seemed the government knew that the pandemic was coming and prepared months before.

While Italy and Spain had very many fatalities, Greece had fared better than almost all European countries. It had been recognized and congratulated for having moved swiftly to protect its citizens.

Online permits meant that construction of the Aetohori house would also move quicker.

Thank God. The stress and headaches of dealing with troublesome local representatives would be over. They would no longer yield such power. The owners of properties would finally be free to complete their projects.

The house at the Aetohori village was to be a "forever house." Not to be sold, but rather be passed down to future generations. This was so that her children and grandchildren had a place to connect to their family roots.

Aetohori (village of the eagles) was the village of Maria's maternal ancestors. She bought the property from a cousin who had no need for it since he had two homes in the village. It was an older home, but not too old. Built in the 1980s.

Maria had moved and settled in her Nisi house by the time the pandemic had arrived in the area. It did not take long for her to realize how lucky she was.

It was much better to live in a house on the hill peninsula rather than an apartment building within the port town. Fewer people and spaced apart. Each in their own home.

Mask rules and distancing, for the most part, were not happening in the port town. This was because many did not believe that the virus was real. And of those who did believe, most did not take the necessary precautions.

To make things worse, those who got infected would not admit to having the virus. "Hush, the neighbors will talk, and everybody would find out!"

This held especially for those with small local shops and services. Admitting to having the Coronavirus might give them a bad name. And that could cost them their livelihoods.

The small port town had become outright deadly, for like a game of Russian roulette, no one really knew who had the deadly virus or not!

The locals did discuss the deadly virus. But the discussions were not about how dangerous the town had become, but rather gossip.

About whom had the virus and lied about it! Maria couldn't believe it.

Soon the deaths started. In the beginning funeral notice flyers were stapled to the wooden streetlamp columns, which was customary. Also, the church bell would ring with a sorrowful tone, announcing the funeral. Also, customary.

All that would soon stop though. For there were too many deaths. If they were all announced people would panic. The church bell's sorrowful tone would have been heard almost daily.

Then, one of Maria's acquaintances died. Maria attended the funeral; it had been closed casket. A sign that he had died of a coronavirus infection. Even so, friends and relatives claimed that he died of cancer.

Shaken up by all this, Maria stopped going into the port town for groceries. She continued going into the harbor town only when needed, mostly for the pharmacy and the hairstylist.

For the rest she drove to the larger town of Nafplion. Along the way and in the town were a few large, air-conditioned shops and grocery stores where everybody wore masks and practiced distancing.

She took her favorite route. A small seaside road that went for a long distance past the Argolis region. Once she was close enough, she turned into the small connecting roads leading inland to the different shops.

Maria started waiting longer for the hairstylist, wearing a headband to hide her grey roots. Maria's hair started turning grey early, in her mid-thirties, just as her father's had.

Soon the hairstylist would not be available because the government ordered all non-essential shops to shut down. Those who kept their shops open faced huge penalties.

Even to go to the grocery stores the residents would need a permission text or slip from the government.

And it would all be enforced by the police.

CHAPTER 2

The devastating fast-spreading virus was almost immediately classified as a pandemic. Governments of every country moved quickly to secure their citizens' well-being.

The crippling fast spreading virus would live up to its name. For *Corona* was, yes, another Greek word. It meant "Crown." And what a royal virus it was!

A Worldometer website was created and updated daily. It reported the mass deaths by country and by district and state.

Even so, nobody had a complete picture of how many deaths the pandemic had truly caused. For some of the deaths were attributed to other causes. Deaths from existing conditions aggravated by the virus were not included in the counts.

In just a few months there was a freeze on sea and air travel. This meant that news crews would be unable to travel to get the stories of other lands. Therefore, many events and deaths went unreported. Especially the ones that occurred in Third World countries.

Then lockdowns began and those who could work from home did. Those who couldn't had to find a way to survive.

Nothing was as it used to be. And as it was with Maria's life, "the world would never be the same again."

THE REMODEL OF THE APARTMENT in Paralio Astros would come to a full stop. Because of the lockdown, there were no workers to be found. Even after the lockdown, workers were afraid to work indoors with others for by now they knew that some of their missing neighbors were not coming back.

The remodel would be delayed by almost two years!

The plan was that with the funds she would receive from the sale, Maria was to buy a vacation home in Palm Desert, in a reasonably priced gated community that she knew well.

She had another option. To get a loan on the rental house she owned in the Palm Desert area and use that money to buy the vacation home.

It was a great opportunity because interest rates were at their lowest. The banks were pretty much handing out money for those who qualified.

However, that fell through also.

Because she had added her children to the title of the rental house, they would have to sign off for her to get the loan. Even if the loan would be only in her name.

Unfortunately, in the United States, you can lose everything you own due to high medical bills. Maria had placed her children on the title as a precaution in case her condition got worse.

She just about worked it all out with the loan agent and her children before flying back to Greece. Then when she called the loan agent to proceed, he told her she needed to be present to get that particular loan!

It would have helped if he had told me while I was still in town. Guess it was not meant to be . . . It sure started to feel that way.

HOME PRICES IN THE PALM DESERT area quickly and substantially increased as the supplies of homes quickly decreased. Probably because the Coronavirus seemed to thrive with cooler temperatures.

Maria could no longer comfortably afford to buy in the gated community she had planned. The homes there went from around $250,000 to $400,000 in a matter of three to four months. And even at the higher prices, they immediately sold out!

SUCH A GREAT OPPORTUNITY, AND now it is all gone . . . Feeling frustrated, Maria pushed her chair back and got up from her desk. She took a deep breath as she went outside. She stood on the balcony and looked at the sea, to the other side of the bay, and then over the vast valley and mountains. This calmed her every time. Even now.

Something else will come up, it always does.

Renting a home in Palm Desert, both year-round and seasonally, suddenly got expensive. To make things worse car rentals also increased. They quickly went much higher. This was mostly due to manufacturing and shipping disruptions.

Car rental companies found it more profitable to sell their better vehicles. They were now renting older, high mileage, and sometimes defective vehicles. Even so, the rental price for the leftover vehicles had increased by at least one-third. That was of the previous newer and nicer vehicle rental price!

On her last visit, Maria had to exchange her car rental twice. With the first vehicle, she heard metal rubbing against metal. It reminded her of an old car she had while in high school. With that one, it was the wheel axles.

Not good. She returned it the next day.

With the second vehicle, the front of the bottom engine cover came undone. This happened when she was returning from an overnight visit to her daughter's house in San Diego.

She first became aware of it when she stopped at a Starbucks for her morning Latte, just before she was to get on the freeway.

When she returned to her car a couple of ladies pointed to its bottom. Maria looked and noticed a carboard box. She thanked them and pulled the box away. Then as she drove and headed for the freeway, she had heard a dragging noise.

When she pulled over to look under the car, she realized what the real problem was. The bottom engine cover had come undone on the back side. She called the car rental company to tell them what was happening and that she was returning the car.

Each time she came to a stoplight, the driver of the stopped car next to her would point it out. "I know, I know." What could she do.

Then something unusual happened. Just before she turned to get on the freeway, she heard a car beep behind her. She looked in her rear-view mirror and after turned her head to confirm it. Still, she could not believe what she was seeing.

The car that was beeping was right behind her and it had no front hood on it! And if that wasn't strange enough, both the driver and passengers were waving their hands up in the air!

Someone was playing with her or maybe giving her some kind of warning. Possibly that she needed to stop visiting her daughter often. Maybe warning her it was not safe for her to do so yet.

Definitely a sign. Maria would have to think about it.

The good thing was that when the car was moving the cover stayed up.

"I paid one third more to get this!" she frustratingly explained to the representative at the car rental counter. The representative remained silent, only shrugging her shoulders as she searched for a replacement car.

Thank God! Despite it also being older, the third car did not have any mechanical problems.

A GLOBAL TREND STARTED TAKING PLACE. People began moving out of crowded cities. They moved into smaller communities where homes were more spread out. Some even ventured into remote areas where there was less of a likelihood of getting infected.

Maria observed that a growing number of people were choosing to stay in the port town for extended periods, even during the off-season.

Additionally, she noticed an increasing number of elderly individuals relocating to their village homes in the nearby Parnon mountain range area.

Maria's mother, who resided in the nearby mountain village where Maria was born, now had more neighbors. She had also made a new friend with whom she enjoyed taking walks and teaching gardening techniques.

The villages were experiencing a resurgence of activity, with some individuals making a permanent move. Young people were also joining in, opting to settle in the villages and pursue agriculture.

There was a noticeable increase in the planting of olive trees, blueberry fields, fruit trees, and vineyards, some of which offered wine tasting. Also, more routes were being added to "the Arcadia Wine Roads" for visitors to enjoy.

Many new home improvements and constructions were also taking place in nearby villages.

All this led to the revitalization of small village "platies" (centers) with new coffee shops, ouzeries, and restaurants opening up.

AND JUST AS THE WORLD WAS BEGINNING to adjust to the effects of the Coronavirus pandemic and regain some stability, another tragic event occurred.

Russia had already positioned military vehicles along its borders when President Biden publicly disclosed that he had credible information indicating Putin's intention to start a war against neighboring Ukraine.

Sadly, this prediction soon came to realization.

The outbreak of war in Ukraine had a significant impact on global energy markets. It also caused a shortage of food, for Russia and Ukraine jointly supplied around a quarter of the world's wheat exports.

Bans on Russian oil imports resulted in even higher oil prices, which were already on the rise due to inflation caused by the pandemic. To retaliate, Russia shut down the Nord Stream gas pipeline, worsening the situation further.

THE WORLD IS COMING UNDONE. Maria was growing increasingly concerned about the stability of Greece due to recent problems caused by neighboring Turkey regarding sea borders and nearby islands. While these disputes have historically not been taken seriously, the ongoing war in Ukraine had heightened concerns.

Besides, just months before, many unconcerned Ukrainians did not believe that Russia would invade, but they were proven wrong.

EUROPEANS, PARTICULARLY NORTHERN Europeans, were bracing themselves for an extremely cold and challenging winter ahead. Some were already preparing to escape to warmer countries in southern Europe, like Spain, Italy, and Greece.

They found it more cost-effective to travel and rent a home in warmer countries rather than paying exorbitant energy bills to heat their own homes.

Many Northern Europeans had now become "snowbirds." A term used in the United States to refer to people who leave their homes to stay at warmer climate locations during the cold winter months. Maria had met many snowbirds in the Palm Desert area.

MARIA REALIZED SHE NEEDED TO change her plans once again. *Or at least tweak them a bit . . .* She was now considering investing in Greece to boost her income.

Unlike Southern California, Greece had numerous real estate investment opportunities, particularly in purchasing and renovating older homes to sell for a profit.

The properties were there to purchase, workers were also available, but the problem was that the process was slower, much slower in Greece.

"Everything in Greece seems to move much slower," Maria sighed to herself.

For it was true, the mentality was quite different.

Whenever she requested something to be done, a common response was, "There's always tomorrow."

Another common answer was, "Today is a holiday." And there were a lot of holidays in Greece, all year-round.

Also, Maria lived in an agricultural area where spring was dedicated to planting, while fall was for harvesting.

The summer was also a problem for many individuals took up jobs in the tourism industry for extra income. Jobs such as small repairs and maintenance for hotels and vacation homes, as well as serving at local cafes and restaurants.

To ensure success in the real estate industry it would require full-time professional subcontractors. Where was she to look to find them? They would not only need to be professional, but they would also need to be trustworthy. And they would have to be willing to work with and for a "foreigner."

Buy, fix, and resell. This was how she made most of her money in Southern California. It was something she had learned well. And she could apply all that she had learned here.

Oh, how stressful. Although it all seemed achievable, Maria couldn't help but sigh at the idea of it. She knew that no matter which nearby town or village she chose for her project, she would encounter both expected and unexpected obstacles.

Yes, her plans had been derailed, and she would need to come up with new ones. However, the more she contemplated the situation, the less likely it seemed that she would pursue a real estate investment project in Greece.

Derailed like pretty much everybody else's. Maria shifted her thoughts away from investing in real estate. Besides, she had her own ongoing projects in Greece that needed her full attention.

And if that wasn't enough, there were some recent concerning events that made Maria cancel her scheduled trip and stay in Greece for the upcoming fall.

Her decision to stay in Greece was mostly due to the recent spate of thefts that took place in the port town and nearby villages.

The thefts were well-planned and organized, with the perpetrators posing as maintenance and repair workers hired by local companies. Once inside the homes, they would scope out to steal valuable items.

It was possible that one of these thieves had even visited Maria's home under the guise of an assistant to the person who installed some new awnings.

Her first step was to order extra locks for her front door and after locks for the small closet and bathroom windows to ensure her home was secure.

She had already installed bars on the door and windows downstairs. And had also a metal sliding security fence for the upstairs French doors and windows, so those were no longer a concern.

Although the idea of not spending the holidays with her children saddened her, Maria decided it was best to stay put.

She made a promise to herself that this wouldn't be the case next year or in the years to follow.

SINCE SHE WAS STAYING PUT, Maria quickly got back to work on her projects.

She contacted her contractor to discuss the completion of the sundeck. Maria wanted him to add a fence and a small ground stone cover layer over the cement as soon as possible in order to create a comfortable outdoor space where she can enjoy the coming sunny winter days.

Maria also expressed her desire to finalize the cleanup at Aetohori, so that the workers could begin pouring the cement for the two downstairs bedrooms and the balcony above them in January as had been planned.

She wanted to quickly finish the upstairs portion of the village house in order to move in. After, she would sell her completely rebuilt and remodeled Nisi peninsula house, which now included a private patio and sundeck, along with the remodeled apartment.

Selling both properties would provide her with the necessary funds to purchase a home for herself in the Palm Desert area. Her plan was to rent it out only during the "snowbird season," from January through the end of April.

For the rest of the year, the property would be available for her personal use.

This was a common practice among the residents in the area since the rental income would cover a significant portion of their living expenses. Some would visit and stay with their families to save some money, while others who could afford it used the extra income to travel.

Maria's projects would soon become stuck again. The contractor started having some problems, both at home and with the workers, which prevented him from getting anything done.

And it hadn't been only him, for it seemed that all of the residents of the port town area were experiencing problems.

Each one of them seemed to be having "a series of strange mostly unfortunate events" happening in their lives.

Maria couldn't quite pinpoint what was happening, but she had heard others say out loud that "something has changed."

She had not lived in the area long enough to experience these events as the locals had. For them it seemed, "what used to be, no longer was."

CHAPTER 3

Early spring soon arrived, and the nights were starting to warm up.

Thank God. For during the winter, Maria wore a thick headband to bed at night as she found her head to be more sensitive after her breakdown and felt uncomfortably cold at times.

In fact, Maria wore a headband all day long year-round, except in the summer, as the warm sun seemed to prevent negative energy from affecting her aura.

By now she was fully aware of negative energy and energy vampires (beings that drained energy from others), and there were a few of them in the small port town.

To her, most people there seemed limited, existing at low vibrations, they also seemed to speak and move very slowly. A few resembled zombies, lacking any emotional expression and repeating the same actions each day, as if they were programmed to do so.

Though she would notice a change in their behavior during the summer months.

Perhaps it was due to absorbing the increased energy from the hot sun or perhaps the higher energy brought by tourists and visitors.

Maria also experienced a decrease in energy when socializing with some of the locals, especially those who engaged in gossip and shared negative news.

She wasn't certain if it was due to her heightened awareness of energies, now that she felt more "awake." She thought that may be the case because she began to notice things within the past few years that she hadn't before.

Or it may have been because she too previously lacked energy, when she had her shop and was spending more time in the port town.

During springtime, when she visited the port town or even only drove by, Maria experienced a buzzing sensation in her ears and her head began to ache.

On one of her visits, she had asked her contractor, whose office was in the port area, if he had felt the same. He acknowledged feeling something but attributed it to the hazy, rainy weather.

That's when Maria realized that it might be an annual occurrence.

As she was thinking this, Maria recalled feeling it much more intensely when she was setting up her shop, a few years back, during springtime.

She was getting her shop ready so she could open it for the summer season.

Then again, she had asked others if they were feeling it, but they had just shrugged their shoulders and attributed it to the weather.

The intensity of the feeling had caused her to stop what she was doing, close up the shop, and go home to rest because it had fogged her brain and caused a headache.

Maria did not believe it had anything to do with the season, or the weather, but rather with some type of energy being released in the port area.

Then another thought came to her mind. *Maybe the port area was an experimental area.*

For she had also experienced other anomalies such as repeated thoughts and what seemed to be projected thoughts. And she wasn't alone, others seemed to be experiencing the same thing.

Maria had read an article about how a decade before scientists at the University of Washington had succeeded in "transferring thought from brain to brain via wi-fi without the use of brain implants."

Maybe the port area is within and surrounded by some kind of "energy bubble." As she was thinking this, some old memories started flooding Maria's brain.

MARIA WENT FURTHER BACK IN TIME when she had felt something similar but much more powerful. It was during the time of her breakdown in Palos Verdes.

She was recalling the incident that had led her back to the small port town of Greece. It had actually been an outright attack.

Maria remembered hearing loud, high-pitched sounds that were causing her head to hurt. She had sensed them in her home and despite trying to escape them by moving from room to room, they seemed to follow her.

Peter had visited and informed her that she was being exposed to radio-frequency radiation, most likely from someone in the adjacent building. To prevent brain damage, he advised her to vacate the area promptly.

Following his instructions she booked a trip on the next available flight to Greece, where she was to stay at her apartment in Paralio Astros and only go for short visits to her parents' house at the nearby mountain village.

Peter had advised her to arrive at the airport several hours before her flight.

Maria had packed the night before so as to leave very early in the morning.

YES . . . I REMEMBER NOW . . . Maria's memories were beginning to resurface.

She recalled how just as she was leaving her condo a pipe burst in the complex and water was flooding the parking area below, where her car was parked.

How she had hurried down the stairs to reach the car and after quickly placing her luggage in the trunk rushed to get into the driver's seat to leave the parking structure before it got flooded.

She remembered feeling panicked when the gate she usually exited through wasn't working. She quickly drove around to the other side of the complex, praying that the second gate would work.

How she pressed the button on her remote repeatedly for the second gate to open. And luckily, it finally did, and she was able to leave the parking structure just seconds before two fire trucks parked in front of each entrance, blocking them completely.

She saw it all from her rear-view mirror while driving away, realizing she made it out just in time.

I almost didn't make it.

She couldn't help but wonder if the incident was just a coincidence, if it was intended to stop her from leaving, or, perhaps, to prevent someone from following her.

She remembered that her upstairs neighbor had also left his unit around the same time and that she saw him in the parking area as she was getting into her car.

Was he there to try to stop me or to make sure I managed to get away? Maria now wondered.

"*I was some kind of under-cover agent . . . so much 'under-cover' that I myself wasn't aware of it!*" She mumbled as she wondered if others had similar experiences.

BY NOW MARIA HAD COME TO THE realization that some of her audit assignments were special assignments with a higher purpose. She had made some connections and was certain that these assignments were not just a coincidence.

For some time, she had the feeling that the frequencies were following her during her drive to the airport. She also remembered feeling them at the airport until she entered a lounge area that Peter had suggested. Although she could still feel them, they were much weaker in that area.

The frequencies eventually stopped before it was time for her to head to the gate for her flight.

The experiences reminded Maria of US State Department officials who had been attacked in Russia, Cuba, and China. She searched for the articles:

- *During the Cold War, the Russians bombarded the US embassy in Moscow with radiofrequency (microwave) radiation for several hours a day for decades.*
- *In 2017, US State Department officials contended that Cuba staged a sonic or some sort of attack on employees of the American embassy, causing a variety of neurological symptoms which include cognitive difficulties and problems with balance, eye tracking, sleep disturbances, and headache.*

- *In a 2018 publication in JAMA The Journal of the American Medical Association authored by a team of doctors at the University of Pennsylvania who examined twenty-one of the US government (Cuba) employees found the patients had suffered from concussion-like symptoms—but without any blunt trauma to the head. The Associated Press reported that MRI scans showed damage to white matter in the brains of embassy employees.*

- *According to a 2020 publication "Distinctive Convergence Eye Movements in an Acquired Neurosensory Dysfunction" published in Front. Neurol, in "late 2016, diplomats in Havana, Cuba, began presenting with a unique symptom complex after perceiving a strange noise and/or feeling a pressure field in their domicile.*

  Complaints of sudden-onset tinnitus, ear pain, and dizziness emerged in late 2016 to early 2017 among diplomatic personnel and their families in Havana, Cuba. These affected individuals often reported hearing a loud, high-frequency, localized sound, and were under the impression that it could follow them in a room.

- *In June 2018, The State Department evacuated several Americans from China amid health concerns about mysterious symptoms arising after unusual noises detected by U.S. diplomats and their families working in the consulate in Guangzhou.*

  After initial screenings by a medical team dispatched last month when the first incident was reported, the State Department has sent a number of affected people to the United States for further evaluation.

On May 23, the State Department issued a health alert for China after revealing one employee of the Guangzhou consulate had reported hearing strange noises and exhibiting symptoms of brain injury. The State Department described his experience as "subtle and vague, but abnormal, sensations of sound and pressure," and ordered his evacuation.

Maria now understood that like US Embassy employees in Cuba, and US diplomats and their families in China, she too was exposed to radiofrequency radiation. Knowing this helped her let go of her frightening past and move forward.

AFTER ARRIVING AT THE AIRPORT in Greece, Maria rented a car and drove to the nearby Holiday Inn where she spent the night. The next morning, she felt more relaxed and refreshed as she continued her journey to Paralio Astros.

More memories were coming back. Maria remembered having to take a different route to get to her destination due to roadblocks and also changing the return date once she arrived.

Oh . . . and all those other strange occurrences. There were a number of strange events Maria was now recalling. At the airport car rental counter, the representative changed her vehicle for a car from a different rental company. Also, the person who had been sitting next to her on the long overseas flight was replaced soon after she took her assigned seat.

AND THE HEATHROW EXPERIENCE! . . . Moreover, she remembered the Heathrow connection vividly. She had missed the connecting flight and had to wait in a long line for hours along with others to rebook a flight for the next day. To make matters worse, she had to spend the night in an old and haunted hotel. It was a harrowing experience, and she thought she wouldn't make it through the night.

But I did. Once she boarded the flight to Athens, Maria had felt much better. All her stress had dissipated, and she felt almost magically rejuvenated.

As MARIA REMINISCED, SHE COULDN'T help but feel as though her memories were somehow connected. Though it all felt like a strange dream at the time, she now realized that everything had pointed to her safe arrival and departure on different times and dates than originally planned.

However, there were still two things that puzzled her: the very long wait in line at the airport and the eerie hotel.

Maybe I was being tested for perseverance. It was the only thing that made sense to her.

After settling into her apartment in Paralio Astros, she drove to Kastri where her parents resided. The village of Kastri was nestled atop Mt. Parnon.

Her parents, who retired from Chicago, moved to the village to spend the rest of their years with loved ones from their childhood.

Maria now recalled how she noticed someone who she believed didn't belong there. For at the time, she was unaware of the family connections.

She and her mother were walking along the main

road near the village center when they heard a banging noise that sounded like metal hitting metal.

The noise appeared to be coming from her father's first cousin's house, Uncle Ari's, which was located just off the main road.

She was struck by the man's familiarity for he looked just like Hans, the warrior she had met in Palos Verdes.

Despite her recognition, Hans did not turn to acknowledge her; he remained focused on his task, repeatedly pounding metal to metal.

Shocked and in disbelief, Maria turned to her mother and called out "I know him!"

She was waiting for her mother to tell her that it was a case of mistaken identity. But instead, her mother went into a panic.

"Keep away from him!" her mother called out.

Her mother's response confirmed what Maria had understood, that it truly was Hans, the powerful warrior.

YES, IT WAS CHRISTMAS TIME—Christmas Eve.

Maria remembered how her young nephew and niece, her brother's children, had been visiting and that their father would be coming by to take them home the following day.

She recalled how she had taken them out to the main square to sing Christmas carols and collect coins from the shop and restaurant owners.

She remembered how difficult it had been for her, for her head was hurting badly, and that she was low on energy, and how people were looking at her strangely. And that many of them had given unusually large sums to the kids, instead of the usual small coins, a few of the shop owners had given them five-euro bills.

It had also been at that time, Hans discovered that he was not German but actually one hundred percent Greek.

Hans had been the son of her uncle Ari, one of twins, and born in the same mountain village as Maria.

He was told how he was given up for adoption at the time of his birth because his parents could not afford to raise both him and his brother.

This was the reason he was pounding metal to metal; metal works had been his hobby. Knowing this, his father had prepared a metal works counter for him on the patio that he could use while on his visit, to help him get over the shock.

Peter probably knew about Han's biological family all along. Maria thought that it was most likely Peter's suggestion to provide the metal works counter.

And it was a good thing for when Hans was given the information, he became emotional and cried nonstop.

Eventually, however, he found happiness in the news, for he had finally found his birth parents and siblings.

And yes, they had been related. He and Maria had been cousins!

To Maria's delight, she later discovered that she and Peter were also related. That their grandmothers had been sisters.

In fact, all three of them had been related from her father's side of the family, her paternal grandmother's side.

Maria referred to this family connection as "The Pontikis connection," after her grandmother's maiden name.

Peter's grandmother had a fascinating life story that spanned many years.

When she was a teenager, she relocated to Black Forest, Germany, to stay with her brother's family. During her time there, she fell in love with and married Peter's wealthy grandfather, who was also a friend and neighbor of her brother.

Unfortunately, this occurred just prior to the outbreak of World War II and due to the Nazi government's discriminatory policies, she was ultimately forced to flee Germany, leaving her young son behind.

Instead of returning to Greece, Peter's grandmother traveled to the United States and lived with family members before remarrying in her early twenties.

This time she married into Maria's maternal family side. To her maternal grandmother's brother, a powerful and well-known attorney who lived in Chicago.

Despite being urged by her family to forget her experience in Germany, she held onto her German name "Greta" as a testament to her identity and personal history.

She also kept in touch with her ex-husband in Germany through secret letters, mostly to inquire about their son's well-being.

Peter had shared with Maria that despite their separation, Greta and his grandfather never fell out of love with each other.

Greta was content with her marriage and had three more children with her new husband. However, not being with her son and the man she truly loved caused her immense grief, leading to severe illness and death in her early sixties.

Following Greta's death, against his children's wishes, Maria's great-uncle had married his true love, Katerina, who happened to be the biological mother of the special boy with the amber eyes!

The same boy who as a teenager had given Maria her first kiss on a park swing, and explained to her that the color of his eyes was called "melissi." And as he looked into her eyes he had added to "always remember that."

Greta's intricate story and family relations proved to Maria that we have a spiritual family and that we take care of each other.

It also supported the idea of the book *The Five People You Meet in Heaven.* That "there are no random events in life and that all individuals and experiences are connected in some way."

Maria stood up from her desk. As she looked out at the breath-taking panoramic view of the vast valley and the bay, she felt a sense of relief and peace as she let go of the rest of the trauma she had experienced.

Finally, she could leave it all in the past where it belonged and move forward without carrying the burden any longer.

With May approaching, the weather was about to become ideal—not too cold, nor too hot. The flowers had already bloomed. Summer was on the horizon and before Maria knew it, the nights would become too warm for comfort.

This was typical of the local climate, with January through April being the coldest and wettest months of the year.

In May, the weather became comfortable, but after that, the temperatures rose rapidly, becoming uncomfortably warm and humid.

Maria found the high humidity during summers unbearable, unlike the dry climate in the desert. The heat didn't bother her as much in the desert. She felt lighter there, and her energy level seemed much higher.

CHAPTER 4

August, the hottest month of the year, soon arrived. It brought with it high humidity, stickiness, and mosquitoes.

The alarm sounded at 7:00 a.m. prompting Maria to rise quickly from bed. After washing up, she changed into a sleeveless t-shirt and shorts, and quenched her thirst with a sip of vitamin water. Then, she headed out the front door to tend to her herb plants on the patio.

Next, she watered the fruit trees and flowers in the raised garden across the street. The trees provided shade for the street and her kitchen window during the hot summer months of July and August.

Once Maria finished watering, she made herself a cup of coffee and sat on the couch to check social media for news and events of the day.

As she perused the news headlines, one article caught her eye: "The Perseid Meteor Shower."

The article revealed that the shower would reach its peak in the early morning hours of August 11th, 12th, and 13th. It also noted that this year's shower would feature meteors visible under moonlight and that, despite the presence of moonlight, the Perseids would be bright enough for many to see with the naked eye.

Knowing that the shower was named after King Perseus, Maria continued reading.

It went on to explain that the Perseid Meteor Shower is one of the most beloved and brightest meteor showers of the year; that people from all over the world could expect to see the greatest number of meteors in the early morning hours.

Maria's eyes went wide open as she read aloud: "Those meteors will be seen as a shower of Stars that seem to rain down from the sky."

SHE PAUSED HER READING AS MEMORIES flooded back to her of climbing the other Nisi hill, located across the bay near the coastal town of Agios Andreas, with the handsome young man, many years before.

Upon reaching the top, where there was a small walled-in church, they stood to admire the stunning sea view. As they did so, he shared some information with her: "In the olden days, the stars appeared to fall into the water."

As they walked back down, he confided in Maria a hidden treasure—huge chains hanging on the side of the hill.

He revealed that these chains were used to anchor ships in ancient times, but a catastrophic event caused the land to shift and the chains to remain suspended from the cliff over land.

The hike had taken place when she was visiting Greece with her parents and young brother as a teenager.

And, in the month of August!

"Oh my," Maria said aloud, *Perseus was conceived under a rain of stars, of course, it all makes sense, the Perseids are the rain of stars he was conceived under!*

Maria read on. "In some years over 100 Perseids per hour could be seen with the naked eye" and that "the Perseid meteors, when traced backwards, all come from the same constellation; The Perseus Constellation."

Ahhh . . . I should have asked some questions!

BASED ON HER RESEARCH, THE HANGING chains may have dated back to King Danaus's time, around 1550 BC, if the once heavily fortified hill was the *Pyramia of Thyre-atidas*, as Maria strongly suspected it was.

This also meant that the fortification of the hill also dated to around the same time.

Now she was wondering if by the stars falling in the water in the old days, the young man wasn't referring to King Perseus's time, 1350 BC.

He must have meant the Perseids.

Maria imagined a shower of stars cascading into the water. Perhaps they had both sat together many centuries before, at that very spot on the hilltop, gazing out over the expansive sea during the early hours of the morning.

She envisioned the two of them seated on comfortable chairs, sipping hot tea, and watching as the stars appeared to tumble into the sea.

MARIA SNAPPED BACK TO REALITY, realizing she had stumbled upon a perfectly timed article that may also relate to the area she was now researching, the Nisi Hill Peninsula area, her current home.

Claudius Ptolemy referred to the region as *Astron* in his book, *The Geography of Ptolemy*, which dated back to the second century AD. However, the area was recognized as *Astra* at more ancient times.

Was it possible that the ancient Nisi peninsula and the surrounding area had been named "Astra" at a more ancient time due to the same phenomenon?

One thing was clear, both names *Astron* and *Astra* translated to "Stars."

As she considered this, she realized that the more ancient town of Astra may have been linked to the founding king of ancient Mycenae, King Perseus.

WAS IT POSSIBLE THAT THE ANCIENT WALLS said to have once surrounded the peninsula had enclosed a palace, possibly a summer palace where he and his family would watch the meteor shower each August?

Maybe an annual celebration or festival where friends were invited to watch the most celebrated meteor shower of the year which lasted for a few days.

Moreover, could the ancient town of Astra have been built during Perseus's reign and named to mean "a rain of stars"?

This would mean that the town of Astra dated back to the fourteenth century BC!

MARIA WAS EXCITED ABOUT THE connections she was making, but she knew she needed physical proof to support her claims. So far, she had found no evidence that the Nisi hill peninsula and the surrounding area of Astra dated back that far.

She was not discouraged and conducted another search. To her astonishment, she discovered a fresh source of information about the region.

The source was *The Dictionary of Greek and Roman Geography,* written by William Smith, LLD, Ed, in 1854. It was there that she found some valuable information that validated her hypothesis:

Although the town is of modern origin, it is supposed that the place has retained its name from antiquity, and that it is the Astrum (Ἄστρον) of Ptolemy, in whose list it occurs as the frontier town of Argolis, between the Lacedaemonian Prasiae and the mouths of the Inachus. On the land side of the promontory towards the river, are considerable remains of an ancient wall, built of large unhewn blocks of stone, the interstices between which are filled up with smaller stories, like the well-known walls of Tiryns. On the other sides of the hill there are no traces of walls, nor are there any other remains of an ancient town.

It had been within that paragraph Maria had found the proof that she was looking for. In the part that had included: *"On the land side of the promontory towards the river, are considerable remains of an ancient wall, built of large unhewn blocks of stone, the interstices between which are filled up with smaller stories, like the well-known walls of Tiryns."*

Maria already knew that Tiryns was fortified during the Bronze Age.

With this finding she had proof that a portion of the ancient walls of the Peninsula dated back to the time of King Perseus's reign.

Now she could also claim that the town of Astra was likely named "in honor of his divine conception."

DURING PERSEUS'S REIGN, THE TOWN of Astra and the surrounding area, including the hill peninsula, were under the rule of Argos and controlled by the Mycenaeans. This gave Perseus the power to build a summer castle on the peninsula if he chose to do so.

Perseus was known to have fortified other citadels, such as the citadel of Midea, which he had named Perseuspolis but later renamed in honor of his son Electryon's wife Midea. The citadel was gifted to them at the time of their marriage.

Αστρα του Αργος, Maria recalled writings that referred to the immediate area in that manner. It translated to "The Stars of Argos." She found no other writings on the Nisi peninsula which may have been called *Nisi* since archaic times.

DUE TO THE NATURAL PROTECTION of the bay, a summer castle would not require heavy Cyclopic stones for fortification, Maria contemplated. *Furthermore, the neighboring Anthini hill, across the bay, was already heavily fortified, adding an extra layer of protection.*

Maria recalled Professor Faklaris's findings on Ancient Anthini hill:

One section of the Cyclopean fortification walls, of ancient Anthini, found on the side and next to the road leading to the Agios Andreas' harbor, still stands and is clearly visible.

The perimeter of the walled hill measures about 1200 meters and at various points there were fortified bastions numbering 21 in total all around it.

Most of the bastions were located on the north and east sides of the fortified hill facing into the sea and towards the bay areas.

Not built by the ancient Arcadians to fight off the invaders, but rather by the invaders to fight off the ancient Arcadians, Maria surmised.

Maria interpreted all the findings combined to mean that the Cyclopean stoned fortified Anthini hill was utilized from the early Bronze Age. She also believed it had existed in the sixteenth century BC, and that King Danaus and his daughters had made a stop there before heading to Argos.

That the fortified Anthini hill, which must have resembled a pyramid from the sea, had been built by and to serve as protection for, "the early Dorian migrants or invaders," as they were labeled by seventeenth century historian William Mitford in *The History of Greece.*

Maria was content with the connections she had established, however, she desired to expand her knowledge on the Perseid meteor shower and how it acquired its name. While researching, she found that Chinese astronomers first documented the Perseids in 36 AD.

It was plausible that they were recorded earlier and considered myths. She tapped her fingers on her desk.

After all, Perseus's conception under a shower of stars was mentioned in ancient texts, suggesting that the constellation and meteor shower were most likely named in his honor when he became a hero and king.

Perhaps we should consider mythology as a form of ancient historical fiction. Maria was pondering on the fact that a lot of what was included in older writings has been disregarded as mere myth.

Maria believed that the constellations of Andromeda, Perseus, and Pegasus were named during the same ancient time as the Perseids, possibly at the time Perseus became a hero by beheading Medusa.

However, Maria had not found any writings that confirmed when these universal phenomena were named or who named them.

The mystery of their origin remained unsolved, much like the burial sites of the members of the Perseid dynasty.

It seemed as though all the ancient writings related to Perseus and his family had somehow vanished into thin air.

Continuing her research, Maria discovered that the Perseids were renowned for their brightness, speed, and long fiery tails, making them one of the most impressive meteor shower events of the year. And that despite originating from the north-northeast of the Perseus constellation, the Perseids can be seen throughout the sky rather than a specific area. Also, that:

- *Perseus is one of the larger northern constellations. It was first catalogued by the Greek astronomer Ptolemy in the 2nd century. The constellation is best known for its annual Perseid meteor shower.*
- *It is also home to the famous variable star Algol, Beta Persei. Perseus also contains a number of famous deep sky objects, among them Messier 34, the Double Cluster, the California Nebula (NGC 1499) and the Little Dumbbell Nebula (Messier 76).*
- *The constellation of Perseus is the 24th largest in the sky, occupying an area of 615 square degrees. It is located in the first quadrant of the northern hemisphere (NQ1) and can be seen at latitudes between +90° and –35°.*

MARIA THEN CAME ACROSS ANOTHER article which stated that the comet responsible for the meteor shower was Swift-Tuttle. This comet was known to be the largest object, with a 16 miles wide nucleus, that passes by Earth. She conducted further research to learn more about the Swift-Tuttle comet:

- *The last time it passed near Earth during its orbit around the sun was in 1992 and the next time it will be that close will be in 2126.*
- *The Perseid meteor shower is made up of dust and debris of the comet as they burn up in Earth's atmosphere, for they are traveling quickly at around 37 miles per second.*
- *Even though the comet only passes by Earth every 133 years, the meteor shower occurs every year when*

Earth moves through the trail of its orbit and that stream of debris which stretches along the orbit of the Swift–Tuttle comet is called the Perseid Cloud.

• *It is believed that most of the debris particles have been part of the Perseid Cloud for over a thousand years.*

• *The famous Double Cluster, which consists of two open clusters of masses and is visible to the naked eye all year round, is located within the constellation Perseus.*

• *Both "the rain of stars" along with the constellation they came from were named after the legendary hero Perseus—a demigod of ancient Greek mythology.*

It was now understood that the dazzling flashes of light in the sky occur because of Earth's yearly encounter with the remnants of the *Swift-Tuttle comet*, which is often referred to as a cosmic litterbug.

The Perseids are small pieces of cometary debris composed of numerous metallic and rocky fragments known as meteoroids, which transform into meteors upon entering the Earth's atmosphere.

The luminous trails we refer to as "shooting" or "falling" stars are produced by the air surrounding the meteors, which are heated to incandescence by the objects' plunge through the atmosphere.

How did the Swift-Tuttle comet get its name? Well, that story is not so ancient. It was named so in 1862, after two amateur astronomers who independently discovered it.

Lewis Swift, a resident of Marathon, New York, spotted the object while scanning the sky with his telescope on July 15th. Initially, he mistook it for Comet Schmidt, which had been discovered a few weeks earlier. However, it turned out to be a brand-new comet. Swift did not formally announce his discovery until Horace Tuttle, an astronomer at Harvard College Observatory, found the same object three nights later. The two men shared their findings, and the newly discovered comet was named after both of them.

ANOTHER TWO MEN, TWO PROMINENT American musicians, had incorporated "the Perseid phenomenon" into their music.

James Taylor penned a song titled *Fire and Rain* in 1968, which was ultimately released in August of 1970. It was named after the meteor shower.

Similarly, John Denver included his personal experience of witnessing the Perseid meteor shower during a family camping trip in the mountains near Aspen, Colorado, in his 1972 song *Rocky Mountain High.*

THE PERSEID SHOWER WAS ONCE widely visible over the ancient Nisi Peninsula area, including over the sea and vast valley area beyond it. However, the present-day port towns' and surrounding areas' lights have obscured the visibility of the meteor shower.

And, yes, of course, it was also widely visible from the other ancient Nisi hill across the bay.

While standing on her balcony and gazing across the bay, Maria reminisced about the young man who had told her about the rain of stars that seemed to fall into the water in the olden days.

Wonder where he is and what he is up to? she had a strong feeling might be spending some of his time at the military base in Palm Springs.

During her last departure from the city, she noticed a sign at the airport that gave her goosebumps.

As she entered the departure gates area, she noticed a snack and coffee shop at the corner, which she had previously not seen. Suddenly, her eyes widened as she saw a large "bee" drawing right next to its entrance.

Above it, in bold letters, the name of the coffee shop read "Buzz on In."

And even though her logical mind told her "No, it can't be so!"

Her intuition told her otherwise.

CHAPTER 5

The ancient port town of ancient Thyrea, over which Maria resided, was today called Astros. Ancient Thyrea was believed to have been completely washed away in the sixteenth century BC by repeated tsunamis caused by the devastating volcanic eruption of ancient Thera (Santorini).

The land where the town once stood, as well as the surrounding areas, were known as *Thyreatidas land* and the bay as *Thyreatis bay* since ancient times.

The town's current name could have originated from the ancient towns of *Astron* and/or *Astra* which were once situated in the area. However, it was more likely that the town was named after the *Estella castle* (Castle of the Star) believed to have once stood on top of the hill peninsula.

It turned out that the forted area had been mistakenly identified as Estella castle and recent confirmations revealed that Estella castle was instead located in the Parnon Mountain range area and the citadel on top of the hill peninsula was built at a later Ottoman period date. We will delve into this further a bit later.

Yes, the town was named after a castle that was never located in the area. This was a difficult pill for the locals to swallow. Most were in complete denial and probably will continue to be so for decades to come.

Oh well. . .

Maria continued her analysis on the immediate area.

During the second century AD, Ptolemy, a renowned astronomer, astrologer, and geographer, mentioned the name *Astron* in his writings as "*a place located just north of Laconic Prasias* (Laconic coast)." Ptolemy's writings included that "*Argious' Astron located on the shores of Argos before [south of] the start of the Inachos river which is located before [south of] the town of Nafplion.*"

It was possible that during Ptolemy's lifetime the region was included in the jurisdiction of Argos district. This was not unexpected as the coastal town of Astros has a his-tory of being alternatively classified as part of Arcadia or Argos due to its location on the border of the two regions.

"*Oh my . . . that may be the reason,*" Maria said aloud.

She was recalling how her prior research revealed that in ancient times there were two streams that watered the plains. The larger stream, called the *Tanos*, flowed at the southern end, while the smaller stream *Charadrus* flowed in the north.

The Tanos River had acted as a boundary between the towns of Argeia and Laconia, thus separating the two states.

However, when Maria looked at a current map, she got confused because the larger southern stream was labeled *Vrasiatis* instead of *Tanos*, and the smaller northern stream was labeled *Tanos* instead of *Charadrus*.

She had reviewed several other maps and confirmed the current names of the streams. The *Tanos* had been moved north to where the ancient *Charadrus* stream once was, and the *Charadrus* stream was absent from all current maps.

It was as though it had vanished.

Maria now had a theory. *Maybe it was done to obscure the borders between the two regions. Possibly at some ancient time so that the boundaries between Arcadia and Argos would go back to what they were in archaic times.*

BASED ON HER RESEARCH, MARIA discovered that the ancient Thyrea area was named *Argeia* around 1300 BC. This encompassed the entire territory. It had been named after the daughter of King Adrastus of Argos and the territory had remained a part of Argos until the time of the Trojan War.

Maybe the ancient Arcadians renamed the streams during the time of the prolonged ten-year Trojan War, mused Maria.

After all, the drawn-out war had left the Mycenean citadels weak and without rulers for some years.

A scandalous act done by the Arcadians to take back their gateway town from the Myceneans, Maria suspected.

It all made perfect sense.

So where was the ancient town of Argeia located, where are its ruins? Maria tapped her fingers on her desk.

Where did the residents live, and wouldn't Princess Argeia have a palace?

"Ah . . . of course! The town of Astra!"

If Astra was constructed during the reign of Perseus, around 1350 BC, then it would have been only about fifty years before the region was named after Princess Argeia, around 1300 BC.

This implied that the town would have still been intact and in good condition.

Maria considered the possibility of a castle, Perseus's summer castle, being located on the land side of the hill peninsula where the Tiryns-style wall ruins were discovered.

If so, this logically would be where princess Argeia stayed when visiting the area.

ON THE LAND SIDE TOWARDS THE RIVER... Maria again tapped her fingers on her desk.

The residents of Astra would need clean water for both drinking and washing. For just as the infrastructure of Argos was devastated a couple of centuries before its time, by the repeated tsunamis of the Santorini volcano, so was ancient Thyrea's infrastructure. Even more so, for due to its sandy bay shores, ancient Thyrea was completely washed away.

Therefore, it was only logical that the town of Astra would be built next to the small river *Charadrus*, that was later renamed *Tanos*.

Yes, the once-mighty *Tanos river* was today believed to be the mere small stream of water that flowed into the sea north of the town instead of the larger, more powerful stream that runs into the sea near the Moustou wetlands south of it.

Wonder how the river nereids and other land and sea spirits felt about that? Maybe, just as in ancient times, they enchant humans and have them do strange things... mused Maria.

The Agios Andreas area was known for the practice of black magic and alchemy throughout the Peloponnese. Maria had heard stories of witches meeting and performing spells in the area.

Maria wondered if some of the anomalies that took place in the vast valley, between the two rivers, the harbor town, and the Agios Andreas area were not linked to the change in the river's path.

Maybe if the rivers went back to their original names the whole area would find some peace and the people of the port town would stop blaming and attacking each other . . . something that Maria witnessed happening often.

Vrasiatis . . . where did that name come from anyway? It was the name that had been given to the large southern river stream.

To Maria, the name sounded more like the Greek word for "boiling."

"*Maybe a spirit joke!*" she laughed. At that same moment the song "*burn baby burn, disco inferno . . .*" came to her mind.

She wondered if the nearby brass Stheno statue wasn't projecting thoughts to her.

Then, another thought came to her. Maybe the port area was possessed by the immortal gorgon Stheno.

Maybe that was the reason a large bronze statue of her stood at the edge of the large port, where the waves crashed onto the large supporting rocks.

Perhaps, that was what the sculptor intended to depict, an under-disguised Steno, lurking in the port area!

They really should change back the name of that river, she was sure of it.

Maria may not have had a deep understanding of alchemy, but she knew from her knowledge of geometry that the triangle was a powerful shape. This was due to the rigidity of its sides, which allowed them to transfer force more evenly through their sides than other shapes. In addition, the triangle could not collapse without breaking one of its sides.

And why was Maria thinking about triangles? Well, Maria was good at making connections, and she had noticed some signs that caught her attention. First, a self-proclaimed "demonic being" had drawn a triangle in the sand with his foot while standing next to her. Then, Maria had noticed that some of the shops and offices had the shape of a triangle on their signage.

She found this all a bit strange, especially because of what the demonic being had done. *There must be some kind of connection, but what? . . .*

Finally, one day it came to her. She realized that both river streams met at the seashore, creating the shape of a triangle.

"Oh my God! . . . The river streams are reversed, and a brass statue of a gorgon monster stands on the seaside of the triangle." That would almost make the port area the gate of hell.

"Oh my God!" Maria exclaimed again, recalling that the ancient name of the whole area was *Thyrea,* which meant "gateway." *"The gateway of hell!"*

Maria got back to her research. One question kept nagging at her: *Why didn't Pausanias record the existence of the town of Astra?* For the immediate area, he only recorded the ancient walls of the Nisi Peninsula.

Could it be that the ancient Arcadians intentionally concealed the town of Astra to keep it unknown? Had they literally covered it up? Or . . . perhaps . . . Pausanias saw the town's remains but was prohibited from mentioning them.

Maria thought the latter was more likely.

She had good reason to think so. It was because she had encountered something else that had equally puzzled her in the nearby town of ancient Eva. She noticed that Pausanias did not mention the well-known and extravagant villa of Herodes Attica, built not long before his visit.

It must have been standing and in perfect condition during his visit, yet Pausanias made no mention of it. Instead, he had mentioned the much more ancient temple of Polemocrates that had once stood in the same area.

Not mentioned at all despite its size and significance. For Pausanias failed to mention an opulent villa that had been filled with numerous statues, art, and treasures and had been likened to a museum.

Maria started to wonder if the reason for this omission had to do with Pausanias's lifetime, the second century AD. She had read of how the introduction of Christianity had led to the destruction of multiple temples.

Perhaps Pausanias chose not to mention the villa in order to protect it and its valuable contents.

Maybe the villa housed some of the statues and other pieces found at the much more ancient temple. Maybe that was why Pausanias mentioned the temple instead. She considered the possibility that Herodes built at that specific location to protect the pieces by moving them from the temple to his personal villa.

She would have to research this further at a later time.

Maria returned to the ancient town of Astra and began to have suspicions. She wondered why the town had remained hidden for so many centuries, with little information written about it even in ancient times. Additionally, she couldn't understand why no significant excavations had been conducted on the land where the town once thrived.

As she studied a map of the region, she finally understood the reason behind it all. She came to the realization that if the town was named in honor of Perseus, then the Arcadians' attempt to rename the stream and reclaim the land where ancient Thyrea once stood would have failed.

For the town of Astra had been located "south of the new border established by renaming the river."

They couldn't have an Argolic town standing on the Arcadia side! The boundaries would again become blurred, and this could potentially have led to ancient Arcadia losing its gateway area to Argos once again.

When the remains of the town were eventually found, they were attributed to the Roman era.

Purposely and incorrectly attributed to the Roman era, just like Ephesus, Maria concluded.

A couple of years before, Maria went on a three-day cruise with her friend. They visited the ancient site of Ephesus.

During the tour, she felt annoyed with the tour guide who repeatedly showed them ruins of buildings and temples with inscribed ancient Greek words on the stone entrance ways, yet he claimed they were built by the Romans.

Maria protested each time, despite embarrassing her friend and frustrating the tour guide. The guide repeatedly referred to each building and temple as "another Roman. . ." Each time the infuriated Maria pointed at them and called him out: "Can't you see the ancient Greek script on the stones?"

She was not at all deterred from speaking her mind.

He kept objecting, but she persisted and demanded an explanation. Each time he had failed to provide one.

After her third protest, he informed her, "You only get three questions, and you've used them all up!"

Maria gave him a stern look and turned away. She realized that it was just propaganda and refused to listen to any more of his nonsense.

It was frustrating to hear someone try to blur the ancient Greek history of the town of Ephesus by claiming that the Romans had built most of it, even though there were still Greek structures and temples with carvings identifying them as such.

To blur the ancient Greek history of a town for geopolitics. Yes, probably a similar thing had happened here. She was thinking about the town of Astra.

And it would all have been easy to accomplish during the ten-year Trojan War. A war that had left the Mycenean citadels in Argos weakened, as their top leaders and warriors were sent to Troy.

In fact, the Trojan War had also marked the start of the decline of Mycenean dominance over the Peloponnese.

Who would be paying attention to a small unfortified town so far south?

WAIT A MINUTE . . . MARIA SUDDENLY remembered reading about the ancient town of Astra in a locally written history book she had purchased while running her shop in the port area.

She bought the book to support one of the three authors who was doing a book signing next door. He explained that since it was a self-published book, they couldn't get it into bookshops, and he was selling it at a neighbor's private patio to cover publishing costs.

The book, written by three authors, mainly focused on local families and Greek independence history, however, the first few chapters provided well-written and interesting information on the area's ancient history and geography, along with related images and topographic maps.

Maria went to search the bookshelves.

Ah there it is! She found what she was looking for and started scanning the first few pages.

The section she was reading talked about the ancient town. According to the book, the name *ASTRA* had been included on historical and current landowner's documents for privately owned land.

This was to identify their land as being located over the ancient site of *Astra.*

The chapters had also included a topographic map of the *"Nisi Paralio Astros"* archeological site which had included the Astra area.

The author had included the 2009 excavation that had been done in the area after an ancient marble Ionic style column base was found on some privately owned land adjacent to the ancient Nisi Peninsula.

He stated that the excavation revealed solid stone walls and the remains of an ancient plumbing system. Based on the artifacts found, the archeologists concluded that the site was once home to ancient Roman baths.

And the excavation was frozen and not resumed because nothing of value was found . . .

MARIA DOUBTED THE EXCAVATION was halted because nothing valuable was found. She searched for an article she had recently read about threats and violence encountered by archaeologists, which had also made the news that evening.

Under cover of darkness in an Athens side street earlier this month, Manolis Psarros, an archaeologist, was attacked as he walked toward his car. It was 8:30pm, later than usual for the state employee to return home from his office in a neo-classical culture ministry building beneath the Acropolis.

"There was a general strike the next day and I needed to get through my files on Mykonos," said Psarros, who has oversight of the Cycladic Isle. "I can remember approaching the car but after that it's a blur," he told the Observer. "All I know is that I was struck on the head from behind with such force I lost consciousness."

So, archaeologists may face great pressure to conceal findings or blur evidence, Maria realized.

IMPRESSED WITH THE FIRST CHAPTERS of the local book, Maria looked up the author's name. She immediately understood why the first few chapters were well written, with thorough research and solid proof.

She had met the author; he was an attorney. And although his main office was in the town of Nafplion, he had opened a local office in the port town, right around the corner from her shop.

CHAPTER 5

A couple of years after moving into the town, Maria had opened a small antique and souvenir shop in the port area as a hobby to keep herself busy.

She managed the shop for approximately five years, but she was compelled to close it down after the minimum business tax was raised.

While still running her shop, Maria went to see the attorney about property management issues with the apartment building where she was residing at the time.

On a busy Saturday morning, the attorney was at his local office, which he often opened on weekends during the peak season. Maria closed her shop a bit early to catch him and walked over.

"Do you have some free time?" she asked him after greeting him.

"What do you need?" he replied as he gestured for her to sit across from his desk.

As Maria began to explain the property management situation, the attorney interrupted her and asked rather loudly, "Who are you and what are you doing in this town?"

Maria wasn't bothered by his abruptness because she too interrupted and asked for explanations when things didn't make sense. Instead, she saw it as a sign of high intelligence and was relieved to find it in the small port town.

It seemed the lawyer was well aware of the local customs and the prevalent traditional male dominant local culture. Because of this, he also knew that this town was not suitable for a capable, intelligent, and independent woman like Maria.

"I CAME HERE FROM SOUTHERN California to recover from a mental breakdown, but before that, I was a certified auditor with a bachelor's degree in accounting and a master's degree in taxation," Maria explained.

She noticed the lawyer's puzzled expression and continued, "However, I am not a stranger to this place. I was actually born nearby, in the mountain village of Kastri."

When she realized that he was still skeptical, she added, "I was born in the small clinic located on the road leading to the village!"

The attorney seemed to be in shock, his mouth had dropped open. Maria couldn't tell if it was because he didn't believe what he was hearing or for some other reason that she wasn't aware of.

THAT WAS THE MOMENT MARIA realized being a woman with experience and credentials from trendy Southern California was uncommon in Greece.

That the majority of visitors to the area were from cities with thriving Greek communities, and they had grown up living traditional Greek lifestyles, influenced by their parents' or grandparents' village ways.

Maria found that oftentimes, these lifestyles had actually predated the ideas and customs of the local townspeople. She too had grown up in such an environment in Chicago.

It was the main reason she left for Southern California at the age of eighteen, as soon as it became legally permissible.

It was unheard of for someone with her background to be living in the small port town year-round, especially for a woman. Many locals were skeptical of her claims as it was common for visitors and residents to fabricate tales in the area.

Occasionally, when Maria encountered guests who were more cultured and sincere, they would inquire how she coped with living in a small town surrounded by unrefined folks.In response, Maria would simply shrug her shoulders, for truly she did not have much of a choice.

She was making the best of her situation, by learning how to run a small business in Greece, taking advantage of what the town had to offer, and getting to understand the local people so that she could use her skills to help them better their town.

The truth was that Maria had always enjoyed a challenge. Her positive outlook on life allowed her to see the good in every situation.

The problem was that despite Maria's efforts to improve the area by attracting more visitors and enhancing local transportation, her attempts were consistently followed by failure. This had puzzled her greatly.

Why were they fighting changes that were clearly to their benefit, that would come at no cost to them and improve their lives?

Later on, Maria discovered that the control of the port town was more complicated than what the locals believed. And, although they thought they had power and were ruling the area, that was not entirely true.

Maria later realized that it was not them; that other external forces were controlling the port area. She also recognized that making changes to improve transportation and attract more people and shops would make it harder for these external forces to continue controlling the port.

During the time that she had been living in her apartment and running her shop, Maria noticed numerous strange occurrences. Following each incident, the locals would begin blaming one another, yet nobody ever took responsibility.

Whatever had happened was eventually accepted and then quickly forgotten.

From the very beginning, Maria had a gut feeling that the unusual occurrences were being orchestrated by higher-ups. The incidents she observed were not only beyond average intelligence, but also required extensive planning and coordination.

Maria was well aware that the local residents did not have the necessary abilities and resources to organize and accomplish some of the mind tricks and alchemy stunts she had observed happening repeatedly in the small harbor town.

It wasn't until a recent Russian hack of a Greek bank whose internal control system had been breached and compromised, some years before, that the reason for at least some of the weird occurrences were starting to make some sense.

The local bank in the port area was where the breach had taken place.

That's what it was all about. It had just dawned on Maria that the commotion she had witnessed before the bank closed was a result of the breach of its internal controls.

Maria had entered the bank to complain about an additional charge of 30 euros following her ATM withdrawal.

Upon entering the bank, she noticed that all the employees had been replaced, including the bank manager. Also, the person seated at the manager's desk appeared to be under a lot of stress, literally pulling at his hair.

When the puzzled Maria had raised the issue of the extra charge, he looked up at her helplessly responding, "I guess that's our current charge."

MARIA HAD NOT ONLY WITNESSED THE chaos which had occurred a few years before, she was also a victim of the recent bank hacks. Her account was completely cleared out. Fortunately, she didn't have much money in the account, as she occasionally transferred funds from her US bank account to cover utilities, insurance, and taxes as necessary.

She never recovered her money, but it was a small loss compared to the tens of thousands of euros lost by many unsuspecting customers who never got their money back.

Regrettably, due to the method used in the hack, the bank was able to shift the blame to the customer.

Right after her account was hacked Maria immediately drove to a nearby town to file a dispute as instructed by the phone representative.

It was then she realized that her money had been transferred to an unfamiliar bank with a strange name located in Africa through an IRIS payment.

Once she returned home, she searched for information on the IRIS payment service offered by the bank, since she had never heard of it before.

Maria discovered that IRIS was a new service offered in Greece, allowing transfers up to 500 euros per day without any charges.

Further investigation on the website revealed that transfers needed to be made within SEPA (Single Euro Payment Area) countries, and "Africa" was not listed as one of them!

Maria was still browsing the bank website when she noticed something very strange. She could not believe what she was reading. The transfer limit was shown at 50,000 euros instead of 500 euros.

"That's insane!" Maria called out.

There is something very wrong here. There are too many inconsistencies and errors. Maria was also recalling the 30-euro charge against her account on her ATM withdrawal years back. It was not an added charge such as normal fees, instead, her withdrawal had been reduced by 30 euros!

The bank most likely lost control of their internal system at the time of the breach years before and neglected to look into it. Now, with the hacks, there was a strong possibility that thousands of its customers' accounts had been wiped out. Possibly tens of thousands!

Maria promptly notified the Bank of Greece, as suggested by the attorney, and also sent a copy of her findings to her own bank. Although she didn't receive a favorable response, she didn't anticipate one.

As an experienced auditor, she understood that the matter would be investigated discreetly.

This was preferable to the possibility of being implicated as an informant, which could result in negative consequences.

The government should never have been allowed to open a bank branch in this area.

By now it was apparent to her that all the citizens of this small town were vulnerable to mind manipulation because the presence of retired military personnel and special agents necessitated controls and restrictions.

The attorney informed her that she had a favorable chance of recovering her one thousand euros, and possibly more, but it would involve filling out paperwork and traveling to Athens for court appearances.

Ultimately, Maria decided not to pursue the matter, but she recommended that others who had lost larger sums take legal action.

ANYWAY . . . MARIA WENT BACK TO the attorney's office and the property management issue.

As Maria was describing the situation, the attorney commented that similar problems were becoming more common in Greece, largely due to the financial crisis. This had left many people in desperate need of money.

Maria did not believe that this was a valid justification for what had occurred. Even if she did, there still needed to be changes made in the management of the apartment to prevent a recurrence of the problem.

After pushing him a bit on the legalities of the situation, the attorney explained that a vote by the homeowners was necessary, and that the majority would have to agree in order to change the management.

This meant that the neighbor had no authority to give the books and management to the handyman. It also meant that his argument that he was not responsible because he did not have the books at the time was invalid, and he remained legally liable.

Maria now had the information she needed. She thanked him and offered to pay, but the attorney refused. So, instead, Maria went to her shop and found an antique wooden key holder box that matched perfectly with a piece sitting on the attorney's desk.

She wrapped it up and brought it to him as a present.

Must be another ancient soul. For Maria had found him very knowledgeable, understanding, and easy to communicate with.

Later, she wondered if he, like herself, was on a mission to uncover ancient truths. Perhaps that was why he agreed to write the first few chapters of the local history book, pointing out the remains of the ancient town of Astra.

CHAPTER 6

The building had been under the management of the troublesome neighbors who had been causing problems since before Maria moved in.

Maria recalled how the husband attempted to force her to take over the accounting of the homeowner's association by bringing the accounting books to her apartment and pressuring her to accept them.

"I'm sorry, I'm unable to do that," Maria responded, pushing the documents back towards him. "My brain processes information slowly, and I have difficulty concentrating. Additionally, my understanding of technical Greek words is limited."

It had not taken long for Maria to figure out that something was amiss, as she had developed a keen instinct for such matters during her 20-year career as a financial and forensic auditor.

Her intuition was correct—money had indeed been missing from the account.

The explanations given were convoluted, and even her vast experience could not prepare her for the shock of the situation.

There were not only confusing stories, but also dubious and unsafe activities had taken place. And some of these occurrences were ongoing and had posed a serious threat.

MARIA FOUND THE COMPLEXITIES OF THE issues in the "Homeowner's Association Drama" were not unlike those of the ancient Greek dramas that were still being performed at the nearby Epidaurus Theater.

Across from her apartment, there were unruly Albanian tenants who hadn't paid rent for months. They frequently fought and were loud, and it seemed like they were always running water.

The owner of the problem unit had given the land to the builder in exchange for six of the apartments, including the one where the unruly tenants lived. These apartments were stacked on top of each other.

The property management neighbor, who had tried but failed to give the books to Maria, gave them instead to a handyman who owned a small hardware store nearby. The handyman's girlfriend was in charge of cleaning the apartment building.

When questioned about why he entrusted the accounting task to the handyman, the neighbor had replied: "I was afraid of the unruly tenants for the husband had threatened me."

To resolve the unruly tenant issue, the husband of the Greek Canadian couple, who had recently bought the unit just above them, offered to give them some money and pay for their relocation to another building, which they accepted.

At the subsequent general meeting, it was announced that the cost of the running water and septic tank maintenance amounted to approximately 2,000 euros, which, along with other expenses, had depleted the building's account balance.

During the questioning, Maria discovered that there was no separate building account. Instead, all the money had been deposited into the neighbor's personal account from the start.

What's more, there was no separation of duties, as the person responsible for collecting the money also made the payments and kept the records.

These findings would raise all sorts of flags in the accounting industry!

A third-floor apartment owner, who was married to an attorney and also managed properties, raised concerns about the financial records of the building. This individual noticed that the elevator was being serviced too frequently and requested to see the bills. Upon inspection, it was discovered that the bills lacked dates.

Maria's head was hurting then and now again as she recalled all that had come up at the time.

SUBSEQUENTLY, THE PROPERTY manager neighbor, who had taken back the books from the handyman, demanded additional funds from all apartment owners to cover outstanding bills, often making threats to enforce payment.

One of the owners refused, pointing out that the

water and septic tank issues were the responsibility of the unit owner and that he should pay for them.

Shortly after, the problematic unit's owner suddenly passed away!

The property manager neighbor claimed the unit owner's death was attributed to a stressful divorce which caused him to have a heart attack. The neighbor seemed pleased with this information. "This means that we can no longer collect from Pavlopoulos."

Another apartment owner reminded him that Pavlopoulos's children, who inherited the units, could still be held responsible for payment, causing his smile to quickly disappear.

Maria would later discover that after his passing, all of Pavlopoulos's units had been sold at very low prices. So low that one buyer had even managed to purchase three of them!

Someone had made a good amount of money from the sales, she mused.

However, the drama was not yet over. The Greek Canadian neighbor who lived upstairs from the unruly tenant unit knew the person who managed the units of the deceased man and went over to demand some explanations and actions about the problems and owed money.

After returning from the meeting, the neighbor confided in Maria, "She would even sell out her own brother, that one!"

Maria could not believe what had followed, for not even in her worse nightmares would she imagine such events taking place.

The incident would be etched in her memory forever as "The Night of the Missing Bar!"

IT HAPPENED IN EARLY FALL NOT long after the summer residents had left the building. At around two o'clock in the morning, Maria was awakened by loud banging noises coming from the outside balcony over her front door.

The sounds were like metal hitting metal, "bang! bang! bang!" and then a loud clanging sound followed, as a metal object fell somewhere on the upstairs tiled balcony area.

Maria was too afraid to investigate at the time, so she went back to sleep, planning to check on it in the morning.

When she climbed up the stairs the next day, she discovered that one of the metal bars from the balcony was missing and was instead lying outside the neighbor's door, the one who had demanded explanations.

She picked up the metal bar that had fallen to show to her property management neighbor. He didn't seem to react much to what had happened and suggested that Maria place the bar in the supply closet downstairs.

The next morning, to Maria's shock, she heard him telling the other neighbors "Stelios is dead, he had a bad heart and died of a heart attack!"

Almost happily, Maria recalled. And he had done the same thing when the owner of the six apartments had died the year before.

Yes, Stelios had passed away at his home in Canada. The incident with the bar being thrown at Stelios' door occurred around the same time that he passed away, shortly after he and his wife left Greece.

Once again, the property management neighbor asked that all the apartment owners contribute funds to cover the building's outstanding expenses. This time he was more forceful. He demanded that each unit owner give him five hundred euros!

Another heart attack and the news announced so fast, the next day after the death. A death that had happened in Canada! How did they find out so quickly? Maria was dumbfounded, greatly astonished and at the same time very concerned.

Shortly after the incident the bar went missing from the supply closet and to this day, it has not been found.

"Who could prove any of that!" Maria expressed her disbelief, knowing that many unexplained events were often attributed to black magic and alchemy in the local area, allowing people to get away with things. Even to this day, the mystery remained unsolved and was likely to forever remain that way.

At a later time, Maria would discover that the heart attacks were caused by something other than black magic and alchemy. Also, that the deaths were not isolated incidents and were not a coincidence. For she herself would become a victim of such an attack.

Maria would not only manage to survive, but she would also uncover the truth behind the attacks. However, again, this would be a story to be shared at a future time.

For Maria the gap on the upstairs balcony, where the bar used to stand, served as a constant reminder of that dreadful night.

For the neighbors, and others, the gap served as a warning of the consequences of complaining about the odd occurrences in the area.

During next summer's general meeting, the management of the building and its accounting books were assigned to a different apartment owner. This owner had a coffee shop in the nearby city of Tripoli and his wife had some experience in accounting.

This, however, did not last long for they both soon faced blame for everything that had occurred before they took over. The negative attention began to harm the husband's business and the wife's professional reputation.

With no solution in sight, they withdrew from their responsibilities and returned the books to the previous managing neighbors.

Maria could not believe it!

The management needed to change hands threats or no threats, black magic or not. Maria was not willing to let the situation slide. Despite the fact that all unit owners, including herself, had to pay for the damages caused, she was determined to fight this injustice. And even though her fellow neighbors shared her sentiment; they were too afraid to act.

Eventually though, with enough pressure from all owners, the books were given to a different apartment owner who managed to survive the transition and had continued to manage the building to this day.

CHAPTER 6

The fortified castle believed to be the *Castello Della Estella* (Castle of the Star) at the top of the ancient Nisi hill peninsula was actually not.

Instead of a Frankish castle that dated to the 1200s it had been an Ottoman constructed fortification, possibly with a castle, that dated to the 1700s.

This mistake was likely due to older scholars connecting the castle's name to the ancient towns of Astron and Astra.

Interestingly, both the port town and the adjacent inland town were named *Astros* (Star) after a castle that never existed on the hill peninsula.

Maria found this amusing as both towns had previously fought over the name, with the port town claiming more rights to it due to its proximity to the hill peninsula.

It had been suggested that a Byzantine castle was previously located on the site where the Paralio Astros castle ruins now stood. However, there was no evidence to support this claim, as no historical sources or findings have been produced.

There were only two identifiable construction phases of the Paralio Astros castle. The first phase was believed to be related to the end of the Second Venetian occupation and recapture of the area. This had occurred in 1715, when the Ottomans had fortified some positions to consolidate their presence in the area, in fear of the nearby Tsakonians, and the return of the Venetians.

The second phase was between 1824 and 1825, when the castle had belonged to the three Zafeiropoulos brothers. They were rich merchants from abroad, and members of the Filiki Etaireia, who returned to the area to free it from the Ottoman occupation.

In 1814, the secret organization Filiki Eteria (Society of Friends) was established in the Ukrainian city of Odessa. Its goal was to overthrow the Ottoman rule and establish an independent Greek state.

The Zafeiropoulos brothers constructed three houses which faced the port with the stones found atop the ancient Nisi Peninsula and also reinforced the walls. These walls have remained intact to this day.

THE FRANKISH *ESTELLA CASTLE*, built in 1256, was discovered not by the sea but instead at an unexpected location on the Mt. Parnon Range.

It had also been known as *The Castle of Oria*, and also called *The Xirokampi Castle*, due to its proximity to the small village of Xirokampi, whose name translated to "dry field."

On one of her drives up Mt. Parnon Maria searched, found, and walked through the castle ruins. Very little was left of it.

That was because most of its stones had been carried away and used to build other nearby structures.

The most prominent nearby structure was the *Malevi Monastery*. Similar to the *Loukou Monastery*, it was surrounded by stone walls.

The *Malevi Monastery* was said to be miraculous. That was because many visitors had reported being healed while visiting it, and there were written records of these experiences.

A wealthy Cypriot couple built the larger church, found within the monastery walls, as fulfillment of a promise they made after their son was healed while visiting the monastery as a young boy. This was the reason the monastery became very well-known in Cyprus.

Tour buses filled with religious pilgrims from other parts of Greece and Cyprus can be found at the monastery year-round.

Malevi Monastery also had a rich historical significance.

Just beyond the main entrance stands a smaller church. An ancient church that dated back to the seventh century.

The small, historic church houses the ancient healing icon depicting the Dormition of the Virgin Mary, said to have been painted by Luke the Evangelist.

According to the chronicles of the monks, they brought the icon over with them when they fled Mt. Athos, during political turmoil in northern Greece, which had occurred in the late sixth and early seventh centuries.

The first monastery was established in 717 at a higher altitude on Malevos Mountain, the same mountain where the monastery stands today.

Tragically though, all of the monks died just a year later due to the harsh conditions. The last surviving monk included the events that led to their deaths, in the chronicles before succumbing to the cold.

As a very young child Maria had also healed at the Malevi monastery, for at the age of three, after choking on a piece of candy, she had literally "died and come back."

Her mother explained to Maria how a stranger had come into town and given her the candy and how they had tried everything to remove it from her trachea and failed.

She had stopped breathing and turned blue, and they had given up thinking she was dead. And then, suddenly, Maria got the hiccups which caused the candy to dislodge.

They stood in disbelief when they witnessed Maria take a deep breath and call out, "I swallowed it!"

However, all was not well, for after the incident, ghosts would haunt her and like the young boy in the movie *The Sixth Sense*, Maria started "seeing dead people."

To her misfortune, their family home was located a couple of streets below the mountain village church cemetery, and every night around midnight ghosts from the cemetery would come to her.

The ghosts would surround her bed and tell her to leave her body and follow them to the cemetery.

"Can't you see them? Can't you hear them? They

are here trying to take me away!" Maria was scared and exhausted, for this had continued every night for over a year.

Concerned relatives advised her parents to take her to the Malevi Monastery, where Maria had also been baptized.

They even offered to take Maria there along with a young boy who had been staying at their home.

For something bad had happened to the young boy also and he too needed to heal.

The relatives would soon start taking both of them to the monastery to heal together.

Maria's aura and energy were repaired after a few visits, and although she remained sensitive to spiritual activity, she no longer saw or heard "dead people."

However, neighbors later told her that ghosts and spirits were still around her and even though she may have been unaware of them, others had noticed them.

ALTHOUGH MARIA WAS TOO YOUNG to remember the visits and the healing, the boy who was a few years older than her did. The young boy was Peter, and he had attempted to remind her during her difficult transition by pretending to choke on a piece of candy.

It turned out that Peter was visiting the village with his great uncle, his grandmother Greta's brother, and something bad had happened to him on that visit.

As an adult, Peter would visit the monastery for Easter while Maria would usually visit around Christmas.

THERE HAD ONLY BEEN ONE time that Maria had visited the monastery during Easter time. It was on Easter day, a couple of years before her breakdown. Maria had entered the small church to light her candles, unknowingly joining the morning liturgy.

She now recalled how a nun had signaled her to enter and close the door, indicating that she had to stay for the liturgy.

Then she was directed to walk and stand at the front of the church. That's when she noticed a familiar face—Peter, who was attending the liturgy as well.

He too had seen her, and he seemed surprised. Perhaps he had not expected to see her there, as he appeared to be in an "escape mode," looking all around in case he needed to run.

He was attending the liturgy with the same relatives who had brought him and Maria there as young children to seek healing.

As she turned her head to look around, Maria noticed that all the nuns, who filled the church, were staring at her.

In response, Maria just looked down and waited for the liturgy to finish so that she could light her candles and then drive to the nearby village of Kastri to visit her parents.

THANK GOD FOR THE GIFT OF forgetfulness. There was only one time that she had a glimpse of what it had been like to be haunted by the ghosts of the cemetery. It was a terrifying flashback. She had seen herself as a young child in bed, surrounded by grey-colored figures. The figures were older and dressed in customary clothing worn by people in the village.

Who wants to remember stuff like that anyway . . .

Maria returned to the historic town of Astra. She remembered that a recent installation of sewer lines on the main road that connected the town to Argos had been stopped.

The road was closed, and traffic was redirected to a smaller side road due to the discovery of some ancient vessels.

An archaeological team came to investigate the area, but they didn't feel the findings were significant enough to stop the installation or keep the road closed.

Again, similar to what happened in 2009, the team claimed the discovered vessels were from the ancient Roman period.

If the Romans built the town, they would have given it a Latin name like Stellas, not Astra.

Why would they give a Greek name to a town they built? They wouldn't. The Romans typically changed the names of characters in Greek mythology to Latin, and not the other way around.

Maria found it strange that all the findings of the ancient town area dated back only to Roman times.

Additionally, the main reason for the 2009 archaeological dig was the discovery of an Ionic column, which originated in the sixth century BC, predating the Roman period.

Maria wondered if the archaeologists claimed that the vessels found under the road dated back to Roman times to avoid disrupting the installation of sewer lines.

Perhaps, it had been a similar reason to do so for the archeological excavation conducted in 2009, to prevent the landowners in the area from having their land converted into an archeological dig site.

"Astra, as in a rain of stars," Maria remarked while standing on her balcony gazing up at the sky, believing that further excavations and research would confirm that the historical town of Astra existed during the reign of King Perseus.

For a while now, Maria had been perplexed by a matter more significant than the dating of the ancient town of Astra. The discovery of Grave Circle A at ancient Mycenae, which contained deep shaft burials filled with treasures, had not been attributed to Perseid dynasty.

This was surprising, considering Perseus was the founder and first king of Mycenae, and the graves were found inside the citadel walls near the monumental lion gate that he had built.

It hadn't even been considered as a possibility. There must be a reason.

Maria speculated that one of the reasons could be resentment towards Perseus for introducing Pelops to the Peloponnese.

Even though Pelops was highly regarded by both the gods and the people of ancient Greece, this was not the case for his descendants. And there were indications that Perseus had arranged for his son Atreus to rule the Mycenean citadel after his own reign.

Pelops's children and grandchildren had been known throughout the Peloponnese for their brutality.

Must have taken after their grandfather Oenomaus, mused Maria. *Ah, that Karma…*

WAIT A MINUTE THERE MAY BE AN additional reason. Maria recalled how Perseus and Andromeda had left their first-born son Perses in Aethopia, and that he grew up to become a mighty king, expanding his kingdom.

The expansion had included conquering the country of Iran that had been named *Persia* in King Perses's honor.

Maria wondered if Persians' later invasion of Greece wasn't a contributing factor of the ancient and not so ancient Greeks to resent Perseus and his dynasty. She did some online research on the Persian invasion of Greece and found that:

- *Ancient Greek writings identified Perses as the ancestor of the Persians and apparently, the Persians knew the story as Xerxes tried to use it to bribe the Argives during his invasion of Greece, but ultimately failed to do so.*
- *The Battle of Thermopylae was fought in 480 BC between the Achaemenid Persian Empire under Xerxes I and an alliance of Greek city-states led by Sparta under Leonidas I. Lasting over the course of three days, it was one of the most prominent battles of both the second Persian invasion of Greece and the wider Greco–Persian Wars.*
- *By 480 BC, a decade after the Persian defeat at Marathon, Xerxes had amassed a massive land and naval force, and subsequently set out to conquer all of Greece. In response, the Athenian politician and general Themistocles proposed that the allied Greeks block the advance of the Persian army at the pass of Thermopylae while simultaneously blocking the Persian navy at the Straits of Artemisium.*

- *Around the start of the invasion, a Greek force of approximately 7,000 men led by Leonidas marched north to block the pass of Thermopylae. Ancient authors vastly inflated the size of the Persian army, with estimates in the millions, but modern scholars estimate it at between 120,000 and 300,000 soldiers.*
- *During two full days of battle, the Greeks blocked the only road by which the massive Persian army could traverse the narrow pass. After the second day, a local resident named Ephialtes revealed to the Persians the existence of a path leading behind the Greek lines.*
- *Subsequently, Leonidas, aware that his force was being outflanked by the Persians, dismissed the bulk of the Greek army, and remained to guard their retreat along with 300 Spartans and 700 Thespians. It has been reported that others also remained, including up to 900 helots and 400 Thebans. With the exception of the Thebans, most of whom reportedly surrendered, the Greeks fought the Persians to the death.*
- *Themistocles was in command of the Greek naval force at Artemisium when he received news that the Persians had taken the pass at Thermopylae.*
- *Since the Greek defensive strategy had required both Thermopylae and Artemisium to be held, the decision was made to withdraw to the island of Salamis.*
- *The Persians overran Boeotia and then captured the evacuated city of Athens. However, the Greek fleet—seeking a decisive victory over the Persian armada—attacked and defeated the invading force at the Battle of Salamis in late 480 BC.*

Yes, the traitor Ephialtes had revealed to the Persians a path that led behind the Greek lines at Thermopylae. This event became engraved in ancient Greek history, and even today, Ephialtes' name is synonymous with the word "nightmare."

MARIA NOW UNDERSTOOD WHY the history of Perseus's dynasty was not well-regarded in both ancient and modern Greece. For Pelops's descendants became brutal rulers of the Peloponnese and later, the Persians invaded and attempted to take over Greece. And while Pelops was only a friend of his, Perses had been his son.

She now also considered the possibility that the Cyclopic walls discovered across the bay, which once protected the Anthini hill, were also being disregarded for similar reasons.

The ancient Arcadians did not care for foreigners who forcefully invaded, occupied, and attempted to govern their land.

MARIA PAUSED HER RESEARCH AND stepped out onto her balcony. As she gazed inland, she looked at the vast valley nestled between the two altered river streams. After, she turned her gaze to inspect the long seashore which created the last powerful line of the "inverted" triangle shape.

THE FOLLOWING MORNING MARIA decided to go for a walk to look over the land side of the peninsula.

The road that led to her house also led to a walking path at the top of the hill, just below and around the fortification walls.

Maria walked to above the spot where the ancient baths had been unearthed and imagined how clearly the stars could be seen a couple of thousands of years ago from the Roman baths, and in more ancient times from the ancient Greek baths.

The west side of the peninsula offered a vast sea view that extended all the way to the shores of Argos and Nafplion.

Maria imagined herself relaxing in a luxurious bath structure on a warm summer's night. The structure had an open ceiling, surrounded by stunning Ionic columns, providing a breath-taking view of the sky.

What a sight it must have been. She imagined looking up and seeing the Double Cluster in the Perseus constellation.

The view must have been even more spectacular mid-August with the rain of stars falling from the sky onto the vast sea and beyond.

CHAPTER 7

The Perseid dynasty lasted for three generations, ending with King Eurystheus of Tiryns who commissioned Hercules to perform the now famous twelve labors.

Interestingly, Hercules, who was Eurystheus's nephew, was also Perseus's great-grandson.

Perseus alongside Cadmus and Bellerophon were great heroes and slayers of monsters long before the time of Heracles.

REGARDING THE MORTAL GORGON monster Perseus killed, the Roman poet Ovid who lived in the first century AD wrote about how Medusa was once a very beautiful woman who was said to have *"stunning golden hair with perfect ringlets that framed her beautiful face, and that her features were said to be in perfect symmetry with her lips being red like the purest wine."*

Ovid had especially praised *"the glory of her hair as the most wonderful of all her charms."*

Medusa was born on the island of Sarpedon. She grew up there becoming a stunningly beautiful young woman who was highly desired throughout the ancient eastern Mediterranean region.

Many suitors sought her hand in marriage, but she refused them all. Instead, she left the island and took a vow of celibacy becoming a priestess of the goddess Athena at one of her temples.

It had been during a visit to the temple that the god Poseidon had seen her and was immediately captivated by her beauty. But Medusa wouldn't yield to him either.

Poseidon was determined to win her over.

He would secretly visit the temple many times, hoping to find her alone. However, each time he found her in the company of other priestesses.

Just as he was about to give up, on his last visit to the temple, to his pleasant surprise, Medusa was there praying all alone.

Poseidon quickly seized his chance and aggressively approached her, demanding her affections. And even though Medusa refused and fought him off, he managed to pin her against the goddesses' altar and proceeded to have his way with her.

When Athena found out what had happened, she became enraged for the act had not only taken place in her temple, but also at her sacred altar.

As she was unable to punish Poseidon, for he was too powerful of a god, she carried out all her revenge on Medusa.

The goddess placed a very powerful curse on Medusa, causing her to fall to the ground. Her beautiful shiny golden hair dropped off and was being replaced by venomous snakes.

And even though her face was said to not have lost its

beauty, instead of charm it would now only inspire terror in those who looked upon it.

Medusa wailed in horror as Athena completed her curse with: *"From now on and forever, whoever gazes upon you, whomever you see, will be turned into stone."*

THERE WAS ANOTHER VERSION OF THE story that claimed Poseidon and Medusa were secret lovers. This version included that they were "filled with passion" while walking through a romantic forest of olive trees near the temple. And that it had been the beauty of the temple and its location which inspired them to go inside and have intercourse on Athena's altar.

This version of the story explained that Medusa's anger towards men stemmed from Poseidon's failure to defend and protect her from Athena's wrath. And that this was the reason why she later turned men into stone when they gazed upon her.

THE THING WAS MEDUSA WAS NEVER an ordinary mortal. Despite being a beautiful young woman who chose to become a priestess and serve the goddess Athena, she was also the daughter of sea gods Ceto and Phorcys, who were off springs of Gaia, the ancestral mother of all life.

Ceto was an ancient deity and mother to a number of monstrous children fathered by Phorcys. Like Ceto, Phorcys was also a primordial sea god.

Which brings up all sorts of questions. Maria wondered why a daughter of powerful sea gods would want to become a priestess of an Olympian goddess and why she was in human form.

She contemplated whether Medusa had always been a monster, waiting to be activated. For if she knew she was a powerful being, why would she choose to serve as a humble priestess for a mere Olympian goddess?

Maybe it was a trick to weaken the goddess. Maybe Athena knew all along. Afterall, at the end, she sent Medusa back to her birthplace.

There, Medusa was constantly hunted by those who sought her head as a prize. Many of them lost their lives by being turned into stone, until Perseus managed to behead her and put an end to it all.

It was said that Perseus would later present Medusa's head to Athena as a token of gratitude, and that she had adorned her aegis (a breastplate crafted from Chimaera's hide) as well as her shield with its symbol.

Medusa's severed head would also become a symbol during Roman times. In addition, Arabic kingdoms used it to protect the dead, guard buildings and tombs, and fend off evil spirits.

Medusa had not been mentioned by name in the Iliad and the Odyssey, however, Homer included that *"whenever Athena marched into battle, she was said to have carried the head of the Gorgon on her armor."*

Medusa was not only a well-known figure of ancient Greek mythology, for she was still talked about even today.

If fact, her name had become synonymous with "feminine rage" in many cultures.

Maria, reflecting on some of her female friends' relationship experiences, understood and accepted the argument that Medusa "had given herself to Poseidon because of love, and at the end had been greatly angered at the betrayal."

Maria did not recall having such an experience. *Too cautious I guess. . .*

I bet Stheno never had such an experience either, Maria was thinking, as she turned off the lights that night, somehow feeling more accepting and appreciative of the enigmatic gorgon statue standing at the foot the hill peninsula.

CHAPTER 8

After returning to Seriphos and ensuring his mother's security, Perseus departed for Argos, for due to his grandfather King Acrisius having no sons, Perseus was the rightful heir to the throne.

Upon learning of his grandson's return to the Peloponnese, King Acrisius fled Argos out of fear of the prophecy that he would be killed by his own grandson.

He wanted nothing to do with Perseus.

This ultimately led to the fulfillment of the oracle's prophecy.

Oh . . . he wanted to make it look like an accident, Maria mused recalling how his grandfather "just happened" to be passing through the Quit's trajectory.

Afterward, Perseus was immediately offered the throne for the kingdom of Argos, which he quickly exchanged with King Megapenthes for the kingdom of Tiryns.

However, Perseus was king of Tiryns for only a short while, for as soon as he became king, he started building his own kingdom, becoming the founder and king of what would soon become the richest and most powerful Mycenean kingdom, "the citadel of Mycenae."

Tiryns, also known as Tiryntha, like Mycenae, was said to have existed as a functioning town from during the Neolithic period, around 5000 BC.

However, both kingdoms reached their greatest power during the Bronze Age, after being fortified, between 1400 and 1200 BC.

The citadel had been named after the ancient Argive prince Tiryns, the son of King Argus and the nereid Evadne (daughter of the river-gods Strymon and Neaera).

The city of Argos was named after Tiryns's father, Argus.

Tiryns was situated only 20 kilometers south of Mycenae and close to the sea, making it one of the most significant centers of the Mycenaean world. Also, because Heracles's difficult labors had been assigned there, the two would be forever linked in history.

King Perseus was said to have constructed a grand palace within Mycenae's citadel walls. Archaeological excavations have confirmed the existence of this luxurious palace. It was located in the center of the citadel and could only be accessed from the south through two guarded rooms.

The palace's state rooms were designed for royal visitors and surrounded a central court, which featured a covered Megaron structure with four columns standing over a sacred hearth.

The much more ancient town of Mycenae, over which the hilltop citadel was built, was named after Lady Mycene, a daughter of the very ancient King Inachus of Argos.

This had been mentioned in the *Megalai Ehoiai*, a fragmentary Greek epic poem attributed to *Hesiod.*

Hesiod, whose name means "he who emits the voice," was an ancient Greek poet who lived in the sixth century BC. Along with Homer, he was credited by ancient authors for establishing religious customs.

According to Apollodorus, Perseus had also fortified the citadel of Midea along with the citadel of Mycenae, which implied that both towns had existed prior to their fortification.

When Midea was fortified, it was named Perseuspolis, however it was later renamed to Midea, in honor of Perseus's daughter-in-law, the wife of his son Electryon.

After their marriage, the Midea citadel became the couple's residence, and it was their daughter Alcmene who would later become the mother of Heracles by Zeus.

Apollodorus of Athens was a Greek scholar who lived in the second century BC and served as a librarian at *The Great Library of Alexandria* in Egypt. He was best known for his work *Chronika,* which was a chronicle of Greek history.

Pausanias had mentioned the town of Midea in connection with Tiryns and the Heraeum. His mention was the only known clue to the location of ancient Midea and it ultimately led to its discovery.

In his writings Pausanias included, *"returning from Tiryns into the road leading from Argos to Epidaurus you will reach Mideia on the left."*

The Midea citadel was today the largest and best-preserved of all of the known Mycenaean citadels.

Must take that turn and check it out. Maria noticed the sign for Midea on the road each time she drove to Athens.

She had found that the road leading to Nafplion and then to Athens was easier and more scenic than the winding road to and from Argos.

Moreover, she had noticed a few signs with names of ancient towns and sites along the way of the Nafplion to Athens route.

One of them was *Prosymna*, where the Heraeum was said to have once stood.

The Heraeum had been an ancient temple in the Argolic area dedicated to the Queen goddess Hera.

It was part of a large sanctuary that existed on the same site.

In the *Iliad*, Homer included an epithet for Hera called *Argive Hera* which had included that the goddess had once said *"The three towns I love best are Argos, Sparta and Mycenae of the broad streets."*

During his travels, Pausanias had visited the sanctuary and given the name *Prosymna* as the town where Hera's temple was located.

Prosymna was said to be an Argive naiad whose name meant "celebrate in song." She was the daughter of the river god Asterion and, along with her sisters Acraea and Euboea, the three had served as "wet-nurses for the children of the goddess Hera."

Maria recalled seeing a sign with that name as she searched online and found a map which had included Prosymna as a village in the municipal unit of Mycenae.

Yup, the town is still there and still goes by the same name. Fascinating. . .

In her research Maria found that in 1878 a beehive tomb structure dating back to ancient Mycenean times had been found in the area of Prosymna by the Greek archeologist, Panagiotis Stamatakis.

She had come across that name before.

Panagiotis Stamatakis had been appointed by the Greek state to collaborate with and oversee the excavation of the "*Mycenean Grave Circle A.*" The world famous 1876 Mycenae excavation, which was led by Heinrich and Sophia Schliemann.

Despite his valuable archaeological work on the site, Stamatakis was not publicly acknowledged at the time, and the Schliemanns were credited as the sole excavators.

In his manuscripts, which are now considered invaluable, Stamatakis had meticulously recorded all the discoveries, along with their exact locations. He had also attributed them to their specific burials.

Although the manuscripts were lost for more than a century, they were eventually found and are now part of the archives at the National Archaeological Museum in Athens, where they are recognized as "a crucial component of the excavation."

It was widely accepted amongst archaeologists that the Mycenaean Grave Circle A predates Agamemnon's lifetime. However, the archaeologists have not gone further to make a claim as to whom they believe the graves belonged to.

If the graves belonged to the Perseid dynasty—King Perseus, Queen Andromeda, and their children—-as Maria believed they did, the question remained: where did the buried gold and riches come from?

Well, Perseus had traveled and made important connections with high-ranking and powerful friends. It was likely that Perseus was rewarded with valuable gifts for his heroic accomplishment. And it was probable that a lot of these gifts were inherited from past generations and held in high esteem by the kings and rulers who presented them to Perseus.

This would clarify why some of the items found dated back to the early Bronze Age, preceding Perseus' time.

Furthermore, the affluent kingdom of Princess Andromeda's royal family was situated in the vicinity of the Nile River, which facilitated the passing of various sea vessels and supported trade.

This trade accounted for the diverse range of objects, some of which were said to have come from faraway lands.

Besides, there was no mention anywhere that ancient Mycenae had been a powerful and wealthy town before the time of its fortification. So, it would be difficult for archeologists to make such a claim, and maybe that was why they hadn't done so.

Maybe one day the archeologists will become brave and make the claim, hoped Maria.

CHAPTER 9

*T*he *Treasury of Atreus* was constructed at the same time and adjacent to the fortification walls of ancient Mycenae. The enormous tholos structure housed an abundance of great treasures. It was commissioned by King Tantalus as a gift to his grandson, Atreus, who was to make use of the treasury once he inherited the throne of Mycenae.

In her research Maria discovered that Tantalus's kingdom, which was the birthplace and home of prince Pelops, was situated at the western edge of the Anatolia plateau in close proximity to the ancient island of Sarpedon.

King Tantalus must have been very grateful for the gorgon's defeat, leading him to offer Perseus anything he desired.

Maybe Perseus asked for Pelops to come to the Peloponnese to compete and win the chariot and become king of Pisa. Maybe what he desired was for the Peloponnese to be protected from future invaders and to prosper, Maria pondered.

Maria now understood why The Treasury of Atreus was constructed at the same time and beside the fortification of the Mycenae citadel. The citadel was intended to be governed at a later time by Pelops's firstborn son from the outset.

This would also explain why Perseus departed Tiryns so swiftly to establish the citadel of ancient Mycenae in conjunction with the treasury. A prosperous citadel that he and his family could live in but not own.

Just like Midea, Perseus must have fortified other citadels in nearby towns for his children to inherit once they became of age and married.

None of King Perseus's sons were ever known to become kings of Mycenae.

Maybe it was a tradition for Anatolian kings to support their first-born grandson's kingdoms, Maria contemplated.

Perhaps this is how Pelops acquired his wealth, not from a father with whom he had a falling out, but from an extremely wealthy grandfather.

She recalled how Perseus discovered the danger of Oenomaus's chariot races through Polydectes' deception.

How else would Pelops have known about the chariot races? For Pelops lived so far away from the Peloponnese and was said to have been much younger than Hippodamia. Probably closer to Perseus's age.

With control of the two powerful kingdoms of Argos and Pisa, and with Pelops's great wealth and careful planning, the Peloponnese was sure to flourish.

In fact, during his lifetime, Pelops funded all sorts of infrastructure and numerous temples across the whole peninsula.

As a result, it had appeared as though Pelops owned the entire peninsula. This was what led to the peninsula to be named after him. For *Peloponnese* translates to "Pelops's Island."

This all made perfect sense. It was as though all the pieces of the puzzle had finally come together to form a clear picture of the situation.

Yes, ancient Mycenae briefly fell under the rule of Eurystheus, Perseus's nephew. However, not long after, Eurystheus met his demise in a battle in Athens.

Probably not an accident.

After Eurystheus's death, Atreus assumed the throne as intended, however he was king for only a short while.

Atreus's reign was cut short due to allegations of adultery. He was accused of having an affair with his brother's wife. In a gruesome revenge, Atreus was killed by his brother Thyestes.

Atreus was known for his fearlessness, and his name in ancient Greek meant just that. For ά translated to "no" and τρέω to "tremble."

If he had lived longer, he would have become a brutally powerful and wealthy king.

Subsequently, Atreus's two sons, Agamemnon, and Menelaus, were banished to Sparta, possibly for their own safety.

King Tyndareus happily took them in and nurtured them. They eventually married his daughters, Clytemnestra, and Hellen, respectively.

Agamemnon would become king of Mycenae and his brother Menelaus king of Sparta.

The two would become immortalized in *Homer's Iliad* as it was their feud with Troy that had led to the legendary ten-year war.

All the valuables found in the treasury that were intended for Atreus to utilize once he became king, were likely safeguarded for the next king of Mycenae, Atreus's firstborn son Agamemnon.

Menelaus must have inherited some of his father's traits for he was a fearsome ruler. It was rumored that his wife, the beautiful Helen, did not love him and may also have feared him, and that was why she escaped leaving their daughter Hermione behind.

It was also possible that Hermione did not want to go with her mother, Maria mused, thinking how attached her own daughter had been to her father.

MARIA BELIEVED THAT THE ancient authors, Euripides, Stesichorus, and Herodotus, were correct in their writings about the beautiful Helen escaping and hiding in Egypt, rather than going to Troy where war was about to erupt. Possibly with the help of prince Paris.

She suspected that the abduction was a ploy to start the war and free the Peloponnese from the brutal Mycenean rulers.

Maria also speculated that the great wealth found in the treasury was likely used to fund the Trojan War, and that this was the plan all along—to drain the Myceneans of their wealth and thereby take away their power.

CHAPTER 10

With the thought of the power of wealth, Maria refocused her research on the origins of King Tantalus's great wealth.

Hmm … let's see, where did all that wealth come from?

Diodorus Siculus, a Greek historian who lived in the first century BC claimed, "*Tantalus was a son of Zeus, and he possessed surpassing wealth and renown dwelling in that part of Asia which is now called Paphlagonia.*"

Geographer Strabo, who had also lived around the same time, suggested that "*King Tantalus's wealth had been derived from the mines of Phrygia and Mount Sipylus.*"

Maria delved further into her research, focusing on the geographical region. She uncovered that the Pactolus River, situated near Lydia, was rumored to be rich in both silver and gold. That it was there that the Lydians had discovered electrum, a mixture of silver and gold, and subsequently earned the title "*The pioneers of gold and silver coins.*"

This discovery shed light on at least some of the sources of the ancient king's vast riches.

THE ANCIENT GREEKS REGARDED Tantalus as the primordial ruler of the mythic Lydia.

Lydia was a mythical land located in western Anatolia that spanned the eastern region of the Aegean Sea and encompassed the valleys of the Hermus and Cayster rivers.

Because Lydian mythology (literature and rituals) were virtually unknown due to the absence of any monuments or archaeological finds with extensive inscriptions, myths involving ancient Lydia were limited to ancient Greek writings.

ACCORDING TO LEGEND, KING TANTALUS was born to Olympian god Zeus and the nymph Plouto who resided on Mount Sipylos in Lydia.

Plouto, whose name meant "wealth," was a primordial nymph and the daughter of the god Cronus.

Cronus was the youngest of the Titans who defeated his father Uranus to become the supreme god. He was said to have ruled during the *Mythological Golden Age* until Zeus overthrew him to become the ruler of the Olympian gods.

IT WAS SAID THAT TANTALUS WAS THE most beloved of Zeus's illegitimate mortal children and the only one to be invited to the banquets of the gods. Also, that he was the only mortal to taste the nectar and ambrosia, reserved only for the gods.

Despite being loved and accepted by the Olympian gods, Tantalus secretly held a grudge against them because they were "gods of a different land."

King Tantalus would become infamous not for his wealth, but rather for his belief that he could deceive the Olympian gods.

This had led to him making an extraordinary mistake resulting in a multi-generational curse on his bloodline.

Historical texts revealed that during ancient times (between 1700 BC and 1200 BC), the Anatolia region (now known as Asia Minor) was inhabited by several distinct tribes. The Hittites resided in the center, the Luwians in the south and west, and the Palaians in the north.

These tribes spoke different dialects of Indo-European languages.

Additionally, there were Hurrians in the southeast, and the Hattians, who were the earliest inhabitants of the ancient kingdom of Hatti.

Each tribe had their own nation and pantheon, and individual cult centers had their unique names for deities.

The result was a bewildering number of deities along with different divine names for each of them.

In some cultures, deities were identified through logograms that represented weather gods, sun gods, moon gods, and more.

According to Hittite theologians, each city's deity had a unique personality.

Special weather gods were also recognized, including those of lightning, clouds, rain, palace, royal person, scepter, and army, all considered separate personalities.

Often, symbols representing these deities were inscribed on clubs and weapons.

Therefore, Tantalus had good reason to be apprehensive and cautious of the Olympian gods. To him, they were just another group of gods ruling over ancient Greece.

ACCORDING TO ONE SOURCE, Tantalus faced the wrath of the gods after disclosing secrets he learned in the heavenly realm to mortals.

The ancient Greek Poet Pindar, a lyric poet from Thebes who lived in the fifth century BC, wrote that "*in one of his odes that Tantalus faced divine punishment after stealing nectar and ambrosia, the traditional food and drink of the gods, and bringing it back to mortals.*"

AS PER THE MOST POPULAR TALE, when the stollen ambrosia and nectar, he had brought back to his own people so that they may learn the secrets of the gods had failed, Tantalus put to action a different plan.

At a banquet—the last one he would be invited to—Tantalus brought with him a special meal that he himself had prepared for them.

In order to test the gods' claimed ability to know everything, Tantalus ordered to have his son Pelops killed, have his body mutilated, and after to include it in a stew.

However, the gods realized Tantalus's intention and had refrained from eating from the stew.

Only Demeter, who was grieving over her daughter Persephone's disappearance, had not paid attention and ate of it. (Unknown to her at the time, Persephone had been kidnapped and taken to the underworld by Hades to be his wife).

ZEUS SWIFTLY PUNISHED TANTALUS for having killed his own son to serve him to the gods. Disgusted by his behavior Zeus commanded that Tantalus face judgment by the Olympian gods.

Tantalus was found guilty of excessive pride and confidence.

The Olympian gods unanimously agreed that Tantalus should be sent to Tartarus, an ancient underworld known for tormenting and imprisoning the wicked and the Titans.

IN THE UNDERWORLD, TANTALUS was doomed to stand up to his neck in a pool of water beneath a fruit tree with low branches. However, whenever he attempted to reach for the fruit, the branches lifted the food out of his grasp.

Tantalus was forever thirsty and hungry, yet just inches away from food and water.

In antiquity, Greeks used the phrase Ταντάλειοι τιμωρίαι or "Tantalean punishment" to describe those who had an abundance of luxuries but could never fully appreciate or use them.

The English word *tantalize* also originated from Tantalus's punishment, referring to the suffering of yearning deeply for something just out of reach.

REGARDING PELOPS, ZEUS URGENTLY summoned Clotho to appear at the banquet requesting she "bring the boy to life."

Clotho proceeded to gather the body parts from the stew to be placed in a sacred caldron to boil.

Demeter had immediately gone to the god Hephaestus in order to replace the part she had eaten of. Hephaestus made an ivory shoulder, and Demeter quickly delivered it to Clotho to include it in the cauldron.

Clotho was one of the Three Fates who represented the three stages of life: birth, life span, and death.

Each had a different role, with Clotho being "the spinner," her sister Lachesis as "the measurer," and Atropos as "the cutter."

The Fates were said to have been the oldest goddesses in existence, with no one able to recall their origins.

They were also known to have knowledge of the fates of the Olympian gods, though they rarely shared this information.

Even the powerful Zeus was said to have feared them for this reason.

THE PUNISHMENT THE GODS ENACTED had involved more than just Tantalus, for they had also placed a multi-generational curse on his family.

Tantalus's daughter, famously known as *the proud Niobe*, had married Amphion who was one of the twin founders of Thebes.

Niobe's pride would lead to her downfall as she boasted about her fourteen children (seven male and seven female), claiming they were more magnificent than the goddess Leto's twin children, Apollo, and Artemis.

Niobe's foolish boast had been included in Bulfinch's Mythology, a collection of tales from myths and legends rewritten by the American Latinist, Thomas Bulfinch.

The book was published after his death in 1867. The part about Niobe's boast read as follows:

It was on occasion of the annual celebration in honor of Latona [i.e, Leto] and her offspring, Apollo, and Diana [i.e, Artemis] when the people of Thebes were assembled, their brows crowned with laurel, bearing frankincense to the altars and paying their vows, that Niobe appeared among the crowd. Her attire was splendid with gold and gems, and her face as beautiful as the face of an angry woman can be. She stood and surveyed the people with haughty looks. "What folly," said she, "is this! to prefer beings whom you never saw to those who stand before your eyes! Why should Latona be honored with worship rather than I? My father was Tantalus, who was received as a guest at the table of the gods; my mother was a goddess. My husband built and rules this city, Thebes; and Phrygia is my paternal inheritance. Wherever I turn my eyes I survey the elements of my power; nor is my form and presence unworthy of a goddess. To all this let me add, I have seven sons and seven daughters, and look for sons-in-law and daughters-in-law of pretensions worthy of my alliance. Have I not cause for pride? Will you prefer to me this Latona, the Titan's daughter, with her two children? I have seven times as many. Fortunate indeed am I, and fortunate I shall remain! Will anyone deny this?

Ledo was angered by Niobe's foolish boast. As revenge for disrespecting their mother, Artemis and Apollo used their arrows and killed Niobe's children. Niobe lost her daughters to Artemis and her sons to Apollo.

Some versions of the story suggest that two of her children, Meliboea and Amyclas, were spared.

Upon seeing his dead sons, Amphion, Niobe's husband, either killed himself or was killed by Apollo for vowing to seek revenge.

Homer's Iliad had referred to Niobe's excessive pride. It included that her children lay unburied for nine days while she abstained from food. Once the gods buried her children, Niobe retreated to her native Sipylus, "*where nymphs dance around the river Acheloos, and though turned to stone, she broods over the sorrows sent by the gods.*"

Other tales included that when Niobe fled back to Mount Sipylus she "*turned into stone and that as she wept unceasingly waters started to pour from her petrified complexion.*"

Indeed, even today at Mount Sipylus there is a natural rock formation that resembles a female face. The formation had been associated with Niobe since ancient times.

Pausanias even wrote about it during his travels, stating that it was known as *The Weeping Rock*, with rainwater seeping through its porous limestone.

In addition to Pelops, King Tantalus had two lesser-known sons, Broteas and Dascylus.

Broteas was a renowned hunter who refused to honor Artemis, which caused her to drive him mad and ultimately led to him setting himself on fire.

He had been devoted to the Great Mother of Gods, Cybele, and had carved an ancient image of her, which was considered the most ancient image of the goddess in his homeland.

This famous ancient rock carving was located near the towns of Magensia and Simylum.

Pausanias wrote about the sacred image and that it had been still revered by the Magnesians during the time of his visit.

DASCYLUS BECAME THE KING OF the ancient region of Mysia and the coastal city of Dascylaeum was named in his honor. His wife Anthemoeisia was the daughter of the river god Lycus. Together they had three sons (Lycus, Priolas, and Otreus).

Lycus became the king of the Mariandynians and welcomed the Argonauts and Hercules with great hospitality. In return, Hercules helped him conquer the land of the Bebryces, which Lycus renamed "Heraclea" in honor of Hercules.

Priolas and Otreus were connected with local settlements, Priola and Otrea, but unfortunately, they were killed on the orders of King Amycus of Bebrycia. Otreus was killed while traveling to Troy to marry King Laomedon's daughter Hesione.

IN THE VICINITY OF MOUNT YAMANLAR in Smyrna, there existed a lake called *Lake Tantalus* with a monument known as *The Tomb of Tantalus* as mentioned by Pausanias. This monument was later transformed into a Christian site and renamed as "Saint Charalambos tomb."

Another monument, *The Throne of Pelops*, was also cited by Pausanias at Mount Sipylus, in the Turkish province of Manisa. It was a rock-carved bench that may have been part of an altar, said to still be present there today.

CHAPTER 11

The *revived Pelops* was an extraordinarily handsome youth that Poseidon grew very fond of.

Poseidon took Pelops along on his visits to the stables of Mount Olympus to teach him how to steer his divine chariot.

Mount Olympus had stables where immortal horses lived and pulled the chariots of various Olympian gods.

The most famous of these horses was Pegasus, the winged horse who carried Zeus' thunderbolts into battle.

Alongside the horses in the stables of Mount Olympus were the *Elaphoi Khrysokeroi* (four golden female deer) that pulled the chariot of Artemis.

ZEUS LATER FORBADE PELOPS FROM visiting Mount Olympus due to his father's gruesome actions of killing and eating his own child, which were considered forbidden in the kingdom.

Despite not being able to visit Mount Olympus, Pelops would earn worship in ancient Greece, unlike his father who was punished by the gods and banished to Tartarus.

Pelops had been called *the illegitimate son of Tantalus* because his mother was unknown. It was believed that one of Tantalus' consorts, Dione, Euryanassa, Eurythemista, or Clytia, was Pelops's mother.

Maria's research of ancient writings revealed that Pelops "*travelled across the sea to Greece to compete for the hand of Hippodamia, daughter of King Oenomaus of Pisa and was said to have been Phrygian or Lydian birth.*"

This had to have occurred in the fourteenth century BC, Maria confirmed recalling it was through Pelops, his first-born son, that Tantalus had been the progenitor of the House of Atreus which dated to 1350 BC.

Maria found it was important to track dates in order to make connections and fully understand ancient events. Without doing so, stories remained incomplete, much like a puzzle missing key pieces.

Maybe lack of support for his decision to go the Peloponnese to compete in a chariot race in order to marry Hippodamia and become king of Pisa would explain the myth of Tantalus serving his son Pelops in a stew to the Olympian gods. Maria couldn't help but wonder why Tantalus chose his own first-born son to test the gods' divinity.

Hippodamia's father, *King Oenomaus of Pisa*, was the son of Ares and the naiad Harpina.

Ares had been the god of courage and war and Harpina an armed spirit of a spring near Pisa. Harpina's name had been derived from the word harpê meaning sickle-shaped sword.

Oenomaus had inherited his father's warlike nature and passion for horses, as well as his mother's tendency to harass travelers.

His name Οἰνόμαος meant "a wine man," indicating his fondness for wine which, combined with his rough nature, made him a dangerous opponent.

Hippodamia, his lovely daughter, was named after her skill at mastering horses.

According to Greek historian and rhetorician Theopompus, who lived in the fourth century BC, Pelops received immortal horses from Poseidon and hurried to Pisa to defeat Oenomaus.

However, due to his haste, his friend and charioteer, Cillus, fell and died.

In his sleep the same night, the distraught Pelops saw Cillus standing over him asking for a proper funeral.

In honor of his friend, Pelops raised a mound where Cillus was buried and built a temple dedicated to the god Apollo, called *Apollo Cillaeus*.

Later on, in memory of his beloved charioteer, Pelops also constructed a city near the temple named *Cilla*.

Homer not only mentioned both the temple and the city in the first book of *the Iliad*, for he had also provided hints about their location.

Although Pelops possessed great wealth, it had not been enough to convince Oenomaus to allow him to marry Hippodamia without a contest.

Besides, despite the potential danger, previous suitors, including eighteen princes, had all attempted the race.

They had all failed.

After the race, Oenomaus would order their beheading and their heads were displayed on wooden columns in front of his palace.

This had served as a warning to future suitors.

Oenomaus had the course all laid out, and it was a long one, spanning across the Peloponnese from Pisa in the west, over the river Alphaeus to Olympia and ending at the Isthmus of Corinth in the east.

The suitor would be given a head start while Oenomaus sacrificed a ram to Zeus at Olympia.

As an added challenge, the beautiful Hippodamia would ride alongside the suitor, to act as a distraction.

Oenomaus's team was made up of a pair of divine mares gifted to him by his father Ares, and his chariot was a special racing type. Myrtilus, his driver, was a master charioteer.

As the suitor sped towards Corinth, Oenomaus would each time catch up with him, then reach over and pierce the suitor's abdomen with his spear.

As with the horses, the powerful bronze spear would never miss its target. It was yet another magical gift from his father Ares.

Now Pelops did have exceptional training in chariot racing for after being reassembled and brought back to life Poseidon had made him his apprentice.

Poseidon had taught him how to steer his divine chariot pulled by large seahorses.

And even though Pelops was initially confident with his abilities, he became a bit concerned upon seeing the heads of his predecessors attached to the palace's wooden columns.

To feel more secure, Pelops prayed to Poseidon for help in the form of the world's fastest chariot or at least some defense against Oenomaus' terrible spear.

It was as an answer to his prayers that Poseidon had sent him the winged chariot of gold and a team of tireless, winged, immortal horses.

Sounds like the whole thing was planned out from the very beginning, Maria mused, *once again, the work of the gods.*

Regarding the race, there were two versions of the story. One stated that Pelops, believing he could not win fairly, convinced the king's charioteer, Myrtilus, to help him and that in exchange for his assistance, he would get half of the kingdom of Pisa.

The other version suggested that it was actually Hippodamia who conspired to help Pelops win. That she had immediately fallen in love with the handsome Pelops and arranged for him to emerge victorious.

In either case, Myrtilus failed to attach the lynchpins to Oenomaus's chariot, causing it to fall apart at high speeds. As Oenomaus was unable to stop the horses, he was tragically dragged to his death.

"You shall die at the hand of Pelops." Oenomaus cursed, as he took his last breath.

After winning the race, Pelops was finally able to marry Hippodamia and take over the kingdom of Pisa, now that Oenomaus was dead. However, there was still one issue left to resolve: Myrtilus.

Pelops soon came to the realization that if he were to give Myrtilus half of the kingdom right away, it would be clear that King Oenomaus's death was not an accident.

He concluded that could not work and decided to dispose of Myrtilus.

Pelops threw Myrtilus into the sea, not long after they had reached the finish line of the race, the Isthmus of Corinth.

As Myrtilus plunged into the sea, just as Oenomaus had done before him, he placed a curse upon his murderer. *"I condemn the family line of Pelops to generations of strife."*

Another curse on the family lineage, Maria noted recalling that the Olympian gods had already placed a curse upon the lineage of Tantalus.

The point where Myrtilus fell into the sea was later named *The Myrtoan Sea,* in his honor.

According to Pausanias, Pelops attempted to atone for his crime by founding the first temple of Hermes in the Peloponnese, for Myrtilus was reputed to be a mortal son of the messenger god.

It was said to have been one of the most magnificent temples that Pelops had ever built.

Possibly somewhere near where Myrtilus had fallen into the sea, mused Maria, for her search yielded no such temple discovery.

NOT LONG AFTER HIS VICTORY, Pelops organized chariot races at ancient Olympia as thanksgiving to the gods and also as funeral games in honor of King Oenomaus, as to be purified of his death.

The inspiration for the beginning of the Olympic games had actually come from those first chariot races.

In addition, Pelops erected a monument to commemorate the unsuccessful suitors of his wife, and an annual animal sacrifice took place at the monument to ensure that these suitors were not forgotten.

According to Pausanias, the last standing column of the monument was shown to him during his travels. He had listed the suitors' names in his writings.

Most likely the stone column found at the entrance of the monument. Maria had found that the practice of etching names and other information near entryways of temples and monuments was common in ancient times, as evidenced by similar etchings at the ancient Delphi and Ephesus sites.

PELOPS AND HIPPODAMIA BECAME the cherished King and Queen of Pisa and had a family of sixteen children—twelve sons and four daughters.

However, Pelops also had a son named Chrysippus with the Danaid nymph Astyoche whom he favored above all of his other children.

This had made his other sons envious.

Hippodamia was also worried that Pelops might pass on the throne of Pisa to Chrysippus instead of their own sons. After all Pisa had been her father's kingdom.

Tragedy struck when Chrysippus was still a young boy, for he was kidnapped by his tutor on his way to the Nemean Games.

The tutor, Theban prince Laius, not only kept the boy as a prisoner in Thebes, but he had also raped him.

In response, Pelops cursed Laius to be killed by his own offspring. And the curse worked. Laius's tragic family story had inspired Sophocles to write his three Theban plays, which included *Oedipus Rex, Oedipus at Colonus,* and *Antigone.*

Not long after his abduction and rape, Chrysippus would die.

The death of Chrysippus was sometimes seen as springing from the curse that Myrtilus placed on Pelops for his betrayal.

And even though some had said that he had killed himself due to shame, Hellanicus of Lesbos (an ancient Greek logographer) and Thucydides (an Athenian historian and general), who lived the fifth century BC, wrote that Chrysippus was killed out of jealousy by his half-brothers, Atreus and Thyestes, who cast him into a well on their mother's suggestion.

The enraged Pelops blamed his wife for Chrysippus' demise. It was said that afraid of Pelops's wrath Hippodamia quickly withdrew from kingdom of Pisa, moving to the Argolid region to live in the secured citadel of Midea.

Ah … the curse of Myrtilus, sighed Maria. Then she considered that the warlike tendencies of Agamemnon and Menelaus may have been inherited from their grandfather Oenomaus,

For, after all, Oenomaus was the son of Ares, the god of war.

CHAPTER 12

During Pelops's reign, the city of Pisa experienced a period of great prosperity.

Pelops soon expanded his territory to include Olympia and Apia, and continued to do so until he became the most dominant ruler in southern Greece.

Ancient writings included that "*Pelops gave his name to the peninsula.*"

THE CITY OF PISA THAT PELOPS RULED was said to have been named after the hero Pisus, the first-born son of Perieres, and the grandson of Aeolus.

Perieres had been the son of Dioplethes, who was the son of King Myrmidon of Phthia and Peisidice, a daughter of Aeolus.

The Myrmidons, an old Thessalian Greek tribe, had been named after King Myrmidon. They were soldiers under Achilles' command in *Homer's Iliad*.

Aeolus was a name given to three mythical characters in ancient Greece, and it seemed that distinguishing between them had been a challenge for even the most experienced mythographers since ancient times.

Pisus's grandfather had been one of the three Aeoluses.

THE ANCIENT GREEK HISTORIAN Diodorus Siculus attempted to define each of these three, but he too became lost in his analysis.

Diodorus was most well-known for writing the monumental universal history *Bibliotheca Historica* composed of forty books, of which only fifteen had survived and been found intact.

Diodorus identified the three Aeoluses as follows:

"The first Aeolus was the eponymous founder of the Aeolian race and the son of Hellen. The Aeolians were one of the four major ancient Greek tribes, along with the Achaeans, Dorians, and Ionians.

The second Aeolus was the son of Poseidon and led a colony to islands in the Tyrrhenian Sea. He was the grandson of the first Aeolus, as his mother Arne was the daughter of Aeolus (son of Hellen).

The third and most well-known Aeolus was "the ruler of the winds" mentioned in Homer's Odyssey. This was the Aeolus that Odysseus encountered. He was the king of the island of Aeolia and lived with his wife, six sons, and six daughters."

Maybe start with the most famous one and work backwards. Bet all three were related and named after their grandfathers, Maria pondered.

The story went that to ensure safe passage home for Odysseus and his men, Aeolus presented Odysseus with a bag that contained all the winds except the calm west wind.

However, when Odysseus's crew opened the bag, hoping to find treasures, the winds blew them back to Aeolia.

Believing that the gods had turned against Odysseus, Aeolus sent him away refusing to offer any future assistance.

Wait a minute, another timely article . . . Maria remembered reading about a new Odyssey movie on her news feed, so she searched for the article and found it:

Movie on Homer's Odyssey
Starring Ralph Fiennes, shot in Greece
by Tasos Kokkinidis.

Juliette Binoche and Ralph Fiennes will star in an epic based on The Odyssey.

An epic movie based on Homer's ancient Greek classic, 'The Odyssey' is wrapping up filming on the Ionian Island of Corfu.

Starring Ralph Fiennes as Odysseus and Juliette Binoche as his beloved wife Penelope, production of 'The Return' started in Greece this spring in Corfu and the Peloponnese, before continuing in Italy, Variety reports.

Fiennes and Binoche are reuniting for the epic twenty-five years after 'The English Patient'.

'The Return' will be released in American theaters in 2024. Credit: Bleecker Street

Bleecker Street, which has picked up the rights to the film, will release it in theatres in 2024.

Variety says that the film is an Italy-Greece-UK-France co-production. Directed by Academy Award nominee Uberto Pasolini, 'The Return' will also star Venice Film Festival Best Young Actor Award winner Charlie Plummer.

Synopsis of the movie based on Homer's Odyssey

Here's an official synopsis for the film, shared by Variety: After 20 years away, Odysseus (Fiennes) washes up on the shores of Ithaca, haggard and unrecognizable. The king has finally returned home but much has changed in his kingdom since he left to fight in the Trojan War.

His beloved wife Penelope (Binoche) is now a prisoner in her own home, hounded by her many ambitious suitors to choose a new husband, a new king.

Their son Telemachus (Plummer), who has grown up fatherless, is facing death at the hands of the suitors who see him as an obstacle in their relentless pursuit of Penelope and the kingdom. Odysseus has changed too.

Scarred by his experience of war, he is no longer the mighty warrior his people remember. But he is forced to face his past in order to rediscover the strength needed to save his family and win back the love he has lost.

Odyssey according to Homer

The Odyssey, like the Iliad, is divided into 24 books, corresponding to the 24 letters in the Greek alphabet.

Within the middle section of the poem (Books 9–12), Odysseus describes all the challenges that he has faced trying to get home. These include monsters of various sorts, a visit to the afterlife, cannibals, drugs, alluring women, and the hostility of Poseidon himself. These challenges resemble those of earlier heroes like Heracles and Jason.

Odysseus's return to his island, however, is not the end of his woes. He finds that 108 young men from the local vicinity have invaded his home to put pressure on his wife Penelope to marry one of them. A stalemate exists, and it is only resolved by an archery contest at the end of the poem, which then leads to a slaughter of all the suitors by Odysseus and his son, Telemachus.

Peace on the island is eventually restored through the intervention of Athena, goddess of wisdom, victory, and war.

In the Iliad, the hero Achilles faces no such challenges, indicating that The Odyssey has a very different idea of heroism.

CURIOUS ABOUT HIS JOURNEY BACK to Ithaca, Maria also searched for all the different places Odysseus stopped. She found that he made twelve stops:

Stop 1-Cicones
The Cicones were allies of Troy, Odysseus attacked them and won, Cicones regrouped with 6 benches being left empty on each ship.

Stop 2-Lotus Land
The Lotus plants that grow there make people never want to leave, 3 crew members eat and are dragged away by Odysseus.

Stop 3-Cyclopes Island
The land of one-eyed farmer giants who herd sheep, home of Polyphemus, Odysseus tricked him by calling

*himself Nobody, Odysseus escapes along with surviving
men by hiding under sheep.*

Stop 4–Aeolus' Island
*Where Odysseus was given a bag of winds, once Ithaca
was in sight the men mutiny and open up the bag, they
end up back at the island.*

Stop 5–Laestrygonians
*Southern Sicily, where giant cannibals destroy every ship
except Odysseus's.*

Stop 6–Circe's Island (Aeaea)
*Where the goddess Circe turns half the crew to pigs,
Hermes gives Odysseus Moly (a magical white flower)
to protect himself, Circe falls in love with him, and they
stay for one year.*

Stop 7–Hades
*A rift in the far shores of the earth encircling River
Oceanus, Odysseus speaks with Teiresias about the route
home, he speaks with his mother and Elpenor.*

Stop 8–Circe's Island (Aeaea)
*Odysseus buries Elpenor, Circe warns him of Sirens,
Scylla/Charybdis, cattle of Helios.*

Stop 9– Isle of Helios (Thrinacia).
*Odysseus and his crew get stuck on this island but run
out of supplies, men eat the cattle, all are killed by Zeus
except for Odysseus.*

Stop 10-Calypso's Island (Ogygia)
Calypso falls in love with him and keeps him for 7 years,
Hermes tells her to allow him to return, after Odysseus
built a boat and begins to sail home, Poseidon destroys
the boat. He was saved by Ino who gave him a magical
veil to keep him buoyant.

Stop 11-Phacia
The daughter of Alcinous (Nausicaa) finds him, Odysseus
tells his story here, he is given a boat to return to Ithaca.

Stop 12-Ithaca
Odysseus arrives home disguised as a beggar; he has to
find a way to get rid of the suitors.

MARIA THEN RECALLED THE 1954 movie *Ulysses* that she had watched many years before.

Despite the fact that the name of the protagonist was changed to the Roman equivalent, she realized that the movie largely followed the story of *Homer's Odyssey*.

However, there were some differences, such as Odysseus staying with Circe for five years instead of one, and the absence of any mention of Calypso, whom Homer had written that he spent seven years with.

As a result of her omission from the popular movie, Calypso was not well-known, and Circe was perhaps more famous than she deserved to be.

Figures, it must have been an ancient Roman spin on the story. For in her search Maria found that Circe's ancient island Aeaea was located just south of Elba Island, which was within view of Tuscany.

THE MOVIE BEGAN ON THE ISLAND OF Phaeacia (also known as Kerkyra by the Greeks, named after the naiad Korkyra) where the royal princess Nausicaa and her hand-maidens discover a shipwrecked man who has washed up on the shore.

The unknown man had lost all recollection of his past and was unable to remember even his own name.

Nausicaa and her handmaidens brought the man back with them to the palace, where he was taken in by Nausicaa's parents, King Alcinous and Queen Arete.

It would not be long before he and the princess became enamored with each other.

He seemed to fall in love a lot, mused Maria.

HOMER'S ODYSSEY HAD INCLUDED THAT the goddess Athena snuck into the royal palace disguised as the sea-captain's daughter. And that while the princess Nausicaa slept, Athena instructed her in a dream to go to the seashore the following day with her handmaidens to wash her clothes.

The *Odyssey* had also included that "*the hero's renown as the destroyer of Troy had quickly entered into the oral tradition of the world through which he traveled and that on the last leg of his return, when he is entertained by the Phaeacians on the island of Corfu, with his identity unknown to his hosts, Odysseus 'rather cheekily' asks the local bard Demodocus to 'sing us the story of the wooden horse'.*"

Homer had continued that, "*so well does Demodocus sing the story of the horse, that tears run down Odysseus's cheeks, and he groans heavily.*"

"*Who are you and what is your story?*" King Alcinous

demanded, witnessing the stranger's emotional reaction to the song.

In the movie adaptation of the story, the protagonist longed to remember his true identity on the day of his scheduled wedding.

He ran out on his fiancé and returned to the shore and gazed out at the sea where his lost memories slowly started to return.

Possibly the truth was a combination of the two, thought Maria.

YES, IT HAD BEEN ODYSSEUS WHO came up with a plan for the Greeks to fake their defeat by burning their camps and pretending to prepare for departure.

And the parting gift; a wooden horse outside the Trojans' city walls as a trophy, was also Odysseus' idea.

THE TROJANS WERE OVERJOYED AT THEIR good fortune and opened their gates to bring in the trophy to the town center.

However, they were unaware that the horse's belly contained 40 Greek soldiers, including 30 of their best warriors led by Odysseus.

Two spies were also hidden in the horse's mouth.

That same evening there was a grand victory celebration. Wine was served generously and as a result, many Trojans became intoxicated, they were seen scattered on the ground.

When the signal was given by the spies, the Greek army emerged from the horse and unlocked the gates for the rest of their forces to enter.

They had returned under the cover of darkness and launched a surprise attack, which involved killing soldiers and burning buildings.

This effectively led to the destruction of the city and put an end to the war.

ODYSSEUS WAS A CLEVER STRATEGIST.

When the giant Polyphemus had asked for his name, Odysseus replied with "Nobody."

This way, when Polyphemus later called for help from the other giants while saying "Nobody hurt me," they would think he was delusional.

They wouldn't come to the cave but instead ignore him or advise him to seek divine guidance.

However, as he sailed off with his men, in an act of foolish pride, Odysseus boastfully yelled out his real name.

This had caused more problems for him, for Polyphemus prayed to his father Poseidon for revenge, while casting huge rocks towards the ship, which the ship just barely escaped from.

If his ship, the Argos, was not specially built to be "very swift and maneuverable," Odysseus and his remaining men would not have been able to avoid the huge rocks coming towards them.

THE ARGOS WOULD LATER PASS BY *The Rock of the Sirens.*

Curious about the sound of their singing, Odysseus asked his men to tie him to the mast while they blocked their ears with wax to avoid being enchanted by the sirens' song.

Seeing that Odysseus found their singing amusing,

the Sirens started mimicking the voices of his loved ones to torment him.

Because their ears were plugged, Odysseus' crew had managed to avoid crashing their ship on the rocks, for they were not lured by the enchanting voices of the sirens.

This was a lucky escape, as many ships before them had not been so fortunate.

Maria stopped reading, wondering if sirens weren't more than simply a myth, for she too had an unexplainable similar experience a few years before.

It happened while visiting the Thessaloniki area with her life partenaire, Paul. Paul preferred to be called *life partenaire* instead of "boyfriend," as he believed they were both mature adults. Maria didn't mind and enjoyed introducing him as such, as people always had an interesting reaction to it.

Paul's brother had taken them to an artsy restaurant located at the edge of Kasandra, the southernmost leg of the Chalkidiki Peninsula, in an attempt to impress her.

They were seated at a table near some large rocks by the sea.

During a moment of silence, Maria heard subtle, sweet voices, calling out to her from the sea.

She tried to ignore them but found herself unable to do so.

Soon after, she felt a powerful invisible force pulling at her from her chair. The force was so strong that Maria had to hold tight onto the table.

She was sure that the sirens, or nereids, or whatever they were, were trying to lift her from her chair in order to take her with them into the sea!

When Paul and his brother realized what was happening, they got up to take her by the hand and away from the area.

That must have been what it felt like to hear the sirens. She now understood why Odysseus had asked to be tied to the mast.

Although Homer didn't describe their physical appearance, sirens have been depicted as birds with human heads since the seventh century BC.

Not long afterward, after passing the straight of Scylla and Charybdis, Odysseus and his crew arrived at Thrinacia, the island of Helios.

Tiresias (Odysseus's mentor from the underworld) and Circe had warned Odysseus to avoid the island of Helios. However, Eurylochus, the second in command, begged Odysseus to be allowed to land and prepare supper there.

Odysseus reluctantly agreed on the condition that the crew would swear not to kill any of the herd of cattle or a great flock of sheep if they came upon them.

Unfortunately, when Odysseus left the ship to go up the island to pray for a safe return home, the crew disobeyed his orders and killed some cattle.

This greatly angered Helios who immediately demanded retribution for the loss of his cattle and threatened to take the sun to the Underworld if he didn't receive full atonement.

In response Zeus agreed to smite the ship with a lightning bolt and cleave it in the midst of the sea as punishment for Odysseus's men.

Even though Odysseus managed to escape, all of his men had died. He managed to swim to the shores of the nearby island of Ogygia.

Ogygia was an extraordinary island. It was enchanted and ruled by the powerful nymph and sorceress Calypso.

Calypso was said to be the daughter of the Titan god Atlas; however, Hesiod, believed her to be the daughter of Titan gods Oceanus and Tethys.

The island's name *Ogygia* meant "belonging to prehistoric times," and the island mistress's name *Calypso* translated to "she who conceals."

Nymph goddesses such as Calypso were said to be amongst "the prettiest ones of all."

Calypso was recorded as the earliest known feminists in Greek mythology for complaining about glaring inequalities among the Olympian gods and herself.

She specifically criticized the gods for looking down on her for having multiple sexual partners, arguing that there was nothing wrong with it and that it was unfair that only the male gods had this privilege.

Moreover, she accused the male gods of sexism for abducting and forcing goddesses to serve their own desires.

Calypso also called out Zeus for kidnapping Ganymede, a divine hero from Troy who was described by Homer as the most beautiful of mortals.

She argued that it was unrighteous that despite holding Ganymede captive against his wishes, Zeus still enjoyed the privilege of living on Mount Olympus and indulging in ambrosia and nectar.

HOMER SUGGESTED THE ISLAND WAS located in the area of ancient Greece; however, it was never acknowledged on ancient Greek maps.

There had been various interpretations and theories regarding the location of Ogygia island on modern world maps.

Some early historians and geographers placed the ancient island northwest of Corfu, making it an Ionian Island of Greece.

Philipp Clüver and Petrus Bertius (both historians from Germany and Flanders respectively) created maps around 1600 AD that supported this theory.

These maps confirmed the Greek belief that Ogygia was the same island as the current-day *Othonoi*, a small inhabited Greek island in the Ionian Sea.

Othonoi was also "the westernmost point of Greece."

HOMER'S ODYSSEY HAD included a description of Ogygia:

"... and he (Hermes) found her within. A great fire was burning in the hearth, and from afar over the isle there was a fragrance of cleft cedar and juniper as they burned. But she within was singing with a sweet voice as she went to and fro before the loom, weaving with a golden shuttle. Round about the cave grew a luxuriant wood, alder and poplar and sweet-smelling cypress, wherein birds long of wing were wont to nest, owls and falcons and sea-crows with chattering tongues, who ply their business on the sea. And right there about the hollow cave ran trailing a garden vine, in pride of its prime, richly laden with clusters. And fountains four in a row were flowing with bright water hard by one another, turned

one this way, one that. And round about soft meadows of violets and parsley were blooming . . ."

No wonder it was not found on any ancient maps, mused Maria. For from Homer's description, the island was more like a mirage to those sailing near it.

In his epic poem, Homer narrates the passionate love of Calypso for Odysseus, which eventually fails, *"even though she had promised to grant him complete immortality."*

Homer depicts how Calypso held Odysseus captive at Ogygia for seven years, but Odysseus remained unaware of the passage of time as Calypso had cast a spell on him.

He included that *"Calypso enchants Odysseus with her singing as she moves to and fro, weaving on her loom with a golden shuttle."*

To and fro like the island . . . Maria added.

Odysseus eventually longs to return to his wife, Penelope, and wishes for the circumstances to change as he can no longer bear being separated from her.

He was described as sitting on a headland crying, knowing he would have to spend another night with Calypso against his will.

In response to his crying, his patron goddess Athena asked Zeus to order the release of Odysseus from the enchanted island.

Zeus complied by commanding the messenger god Hermes to tell Calypso to set Odysseus free, as it was not his destiny to live with her forever.

To this message, Calypso playfully replied: "*how the gods hate goddesses having affairs with mortals.*"

At Zeus's request, Calypso provided Odysseus with an axe, a drill, and an adze so he could build himself a boat. Additionally, she provided him with wine, bread, clothing, and some necessary materials.

She then led him to a nearby island where there were trees that he could chop down and use to make planks for his boat.

Odysseus quickly began building the boat, and after he finished, Calypso set the wind at his back.

As he sailed away, she called out to him, "*How dare you defy Poseidon's wrath!*"

According to a fragment from the Catalogue of Women, attributed to Hesiod, Calypso had detained Odysseus for all those years as a favor to Poseidon, who detested him for blinding his son Polyphemus.

Not long after Odysseus departed from Ogygia, Poseidon spotted him and conjured a fierce sea storm causing his shipwreck.

Having survived Poseidon's wrath was how Odysseus washed up on the island of Phaeacia, which was not far from his home island Ithaca.

Upon returning to his palace, he discovered that over one hundred young men had invaded it, putting pressure on his wife Penelope to marry one of them.

Odysseus had disguised himself as a beggar, allowing him to assess his household and test the loyalty of people around him without being recognized.

He was so well-disguised that even his wife Penelope failed to recognize him.

On his way out, Odysseus stopped to pet his old hunting dog Argos, who had recognized him and walked over to greet him.

MARIA STOPPED READING, FOR SHE made an important connection. *Hmmm, Odysseus named both his dog and ship Argos . . .*

She had discovered in previous research that the district of *Kynouria*, situated in eastern Peloponnese, derived its name from *Kynos Argos* which meant "swift dog."

This name was fitting as the residents of Kynouria, known as the *Kynourioi*, had been hunters since ancient times.

Therefore, it can be inferred that *Argos* meant "swift."

NOW BACK TO ITHACA . . . Early next morning, the archery contest was staged and ready to begin.

Homer's Odyssey included that: *"A stalemate exists, and it is only resolved by an archery contest at the end of the poem, which then lead to a slaughter of all the suitors by Odysseus and his son Telemachus and peace on the island would be eventually restored through the intervention of Athena, 'goddess of wisdom, victory, and war.'"*

IT WAS WIDELY AGREED THAT Odysseus was "the true conqueror of Troy," due to his creative thinking, which led to the idea of the wooden horse gift.

Also, he had shown great courage by going into the horse along with the other men.

Odysseus's role in breaking the siege at Troy was a precursor to breaking the siege in his own palace in Ithaca, both accomplished in a kind of disguise.

As a result, Odysseus became famously known as, *The Breaker of Sieges.*

His heroism was characterized by two elements: his cunning intelligence and his bravery in dark and confined spaces.

THE ODYSSEY WAS CONSIDERED a classic tale that highlighted the importance of love, family, and home, over the passage of time.

Yes, Maria agreed, for she could relate to it.

She empathized with Odysseus, believing that he was chosen for his journey, just as she had been for her own.

Maria's life had also been tumultuous, much like that of Odysseus, for she too had lost some of her memories, while others were temporarily erased and would resurface at times.

And, she too had been away for over ten years and still yearned to find her way back home—to her *Ithaca*, to her children and friends.

CHAPTER 13

Maria returned from her Odyssey detour and resumed her study of the founding of the city of Pisa and the confusion surrounding Aeolus.

She had already found that the city was named after *the hero Pisus*, a grandson of Aeolus and the son of Perieres.

Since Pelops lived before the Trojan War, the applicable Aeolus could not be the third one. Therefore, it would have to be either the first or second Aeolus included in Diodorus Siculus's analysis, Maria speculated.

The first Aeolus was said to be the son of Hellen and the founder of the Aeolian race. His name originated from the Greek term αἴολος meaning "quick and light in movement."

Quick movement seemed to be a significant attribute in ancient times, Maria noted.

Hellen (Ἕλλην) was the forefather of the Hellenes. He was said to be the son of either Deucalion or Zeus and Pyrrha.

Hellen had three sons: "Dorus, Xuthus, and Aeolus," and each of his sons were said to have established a primary tribe of Greece.

Dorus ... maybe the Dorians had been named after him, wondered Maria.

After researching, she found that Dorus's (Δῶρος) name was derived from "doron" or "gift."

Dorus was considered the founder of the Dorians who were one of the four major ethnic groups into which the Hellenes of Classical Greece divided themselves, along with the Aeolians, Achaeans, and Ionians.

The earliest literary mention of the Dorians was in the Odyssey, where it was mentioned that they inhabited the island of Crete.

REGARDING XUTHUS (Ξοῦθος), the other son of Hellen, Maria found that he was a Phthian prince who became a king of the Peloponnese.

According to Greek mythology, he was the ancestor and founder, through his sons, of the Achaean and Ionian nations.

Very ancient indeed. Maria had not previously encountered a King Xuthus of the Peloponnese in her research.

THE HELLENES WERE AN ARCHAIC ethnic group and nation indigenous to the Eastern Mediterranean and the Black Sea regions, namely Greece, Cyprus, Albania, Italy, Turkey, Egypt, and, to a lesser extent some other countries surrounding the Mediterranean Sea.

However, although Greek colonies and communities were established on the shores of the Mediterranean and the Black Seas, the Greek people themselves were centered mainly on the Aegean and Ionian seas.

Even today, the Greeks refer to themselves as Hellenes (Ἕλληνες), using their ancient name, and call their country Hellada (Ἑλλάδα), instead of using the Roman-origin names of Greeks and Greece.

At ancient times the term *Graecus* which was derived from the Latin word *Graecians*, was used to refer to "the Hellenic people living westwards of Hellada."

This was also mentioned by Homer.

The Aeolians were one of the four major tribes in which Greeks divided themselves in very ancient times, along with the Achaeans, Dorians, and Ionians.

Originating in Thessaly, the Aeolians were the most numerous, amongst the other Hellenic tribes of early times.

The Aeolian people also lived in other parts of Greece, such as Aetolia, Locris, Corinth, Elis, and Messinia.

According to Herodotus, the Aeolians were previously called Pelasgians.

If the Aeolian people found in the Elis and Messinia regions were similar to the Pelasgians that King Arcas had organized to create ancient Arcadia, they too must have been an unorganized tribe of people, mused Maria.

Hmmm … a bit too ancient.

This made the second Aeolis, son of Arne who was the daughter of Aeolus (son of Hellen) the most likely candidate for the founding of the city of Pisa.

Aeolis had a twin brother named Boeotus.

The Boeotians had been "a subgroup" of the Aeolians that were driven out from Thessaly by the Thessalians Central Greece, which led to the creation of the regional unit of Boeotia.

So, the Boeotians, a subgroup of the Aeolians had been named after the second Aeolus's twin brother, pondered Maria.

Confusing indeed.

THE STORY WENT THAT ARNE disclosed to her father that she was pregnant with the god Poseidon's child. However, her father (the first Aeolus) did not believe her and handed her over to Metapontus, king of the island of Icaria.

When the twins, Aeolus and Boeotus were born, King Metapontus promised Arne that they would be well taken care of and that he would raise them as his own.

That's a strange arrangement, thought Maria. She did a bit of research and discovered that King Metapontus was childless.

As the twins grew older, their stepmother, Queen Autolyte, became jealous of the beautiful Arne and feared losing her position as Queen.

In order to protect their mother, Boeotus and Aeolus killed Autolyte and after fled Icaria to escape King Metapontus's wrath.

According to ancient writings, the two brothers went their separate ways after leaving their homeland.

Boeotus traveled to southern Thessaly along with his mother Arne and founded Boeotia.

Aeolus had instead gone to a group of islands located in the Tyrrhenian Sea, which were later named "the Aeolian Islands" in his honor.

THE TYRRHENIAN SEA WAS A PART of the Mediterranean Sea, situated off the southwestern coast of Italy that was named after the Tyrrhenian people who were associated with the Etruscans of Italy.

Tyrrhenians was the name used by ancient Greek authors to refer to "non-Greek people."

Aeolus resided on one of the Aeolian Islands, most likely Lipari, as he was believed to have founded the town of Lipari, which was the main town of today's Island of Lipari.

Lipari was the largest of the Aeolian Islands, situated just off the northern coast of Sicily.

The islands were named after Aeolus, the mythical ruler of the winds, and the inhabitants of these islands were known as the Aeolians.

ACCORDING TO LOCAL HISTORY, Aeolian settlers from Mycenaean Greece migrated to the islands during the early Bronze Age, naming them after themselves.

These settlers had already built colonies in Metapontum, Italy, and utilized these islands as outposts to manage the trading routes through the Strait of Messina.

Today, Lipari was a municipality in Italy that comprises six of the seven Aeolian Islands: Lipari, Vulcano, Panarea, Stromboli, Filicudi, and Alicudi. Salina is the second-largest island in the group and the seventh island in the archipelago.

MARIA GOT BUSY MAKING CONNECTIONS for the founding of Pisa.

"*Hmmm … New settlers of Aeolian origin from Mycenaean Greece,*" Maria mumbled as she continued her research.

Perieres had been the king of Messene.

His name meant "overly bold" and he had fathered many children. The list included, Pisus, Borus, Halirrhothius, Leucippus, Tyndareus, Deidameia, Aphareus, Icarius, Oebalus, and Polydora.

Ancient Messene was a city in southwestern Peloponnese. It still existed today.

Perhaps Pisus was Perieres' first-born son, Maria wondered, as his name was first on the list. She searched for more information about "Pisus" but found nothing except that he was some kind of hero, and that the city of Pisa was named after him.

Maria then remembered another Pisa, but this time in Tuscany of Italy—the city that is famous for its leaning tower.

She wondered if there was any connection between the two.

While doing further research she discovered that the city of Pisa (of Italy) had a rich historical background.

It was known for its strategic location, close to both the river Arno and the sea, and although the origin of its name remained a mystery, it was believed to have existed before the arrival of the ancient Romans, Carthaginians, and Greeks.

Maria speculated whether the city could have been named after the same person who was known as "the hero Pisus," since his grandfather was the second Aeolus, who had the Aeolian Islands named after him.

According to legend, "the city of Pisa (Italy) was founded by Greek refugees who escaped from a settlement that shared the same name, which was destroyed in the sixth century BC."

These refugees accidentally reached the shores of the Tyrrhenian Sea and established a new settlement, giving birth to the city of Pisa.

Maybe during the height of the Olympic games, Pisa of the Peloponnese had been destroyed. Maria recalled reading that there had been some disagreements between surrounding towns of ancient Olympia.

As she researched, she discovered that Pausanias claimed to have found the site of ancient Pisa, which had been converted into a vineyard during his time, the second century AD.

This kind of agreed with the Italian Pisa legend for Pausanias did not mention ancient structure ruins.

Maria continued her research and found that the exact location of ancient Pisa was well known to Pindar, an ancient lyric poet, and Herodotus, an ancient historian and geographer.

Pindar referred to the ancient city of Pisa as Olympia, and Herodotus referred to Pisa and Olympia *"as the same point when calculating the distance from the altar of the twelve gods at Athens."*

So, what they are saying is that during their time, the fifth century BC, a separate city of Pisa no longer existed. It was the only explanation for distance calculations to be considered "as the same point" as Olympia.

This also matched the Italian Pisa legend that *"the Greek refugees' homonymous settlement was destroyed in the sixth century BC."*

"Puzzle solved!"

IN ANCIENT TIMES, the city of Pisa (of the Peloponnese) was celebrated as the residence of King Oenomaus and after the residence of King Pelops.

So, what happened to Pisus? Did he live long enough to become the first king of Pisa? Did he die at a young age? Long enough to become a hero though . . . Wonder what task he accomplished to become one? Were the thoughts going through Maria's mind.

Then Maria got the goosepimples.

"Perhaps Oenomaus killed him and that's how he became the king of Pisa," she mumbled. It was very possible because even the dates made sense.

THAT IS ENOUGH WORK FOR TODAY. Maria decided to take a break.

As she gazed at the hill across the bay, her mind drifted back to the time when she climbed that hill with a young man who had amber eyes.

She had recognized him from the time they used to live across the street from each other in Chicago.

Then her thoughts, each time, without fail, would go to wondering where he was and what he was doing at the moment. Though by now, she instinctively knew the answer for she had been given signs that he was still around, on important assignments in far-off lands.

Maria felt safe, even amidst the chaos that surrounded her, for both he and Peter had been a constant presence in her life. And, aside from their important assignments, they always made sure to check on her.

Hopefully we will soon meet again in Southern California, was the next thought that came to Maria as she got ready for bed.

She was also missing her children.

Patience. Soon enough I will buy that home in Palm Desert.

She remembered a response from a divine source during her toughest times, when she was at her lowest point: "*Perseverance requires faith, hope and patience.*"

Maria had the faith and hope parts covered but was lacking patience.

"*Perhaps this is my test,*" Maria mumbled as she drifted off to sleep, "*a test of patience.*"

CHAPTER 14

Maria started her morning by making coffee and checking her emails and news posts. After that, she resumed her research on Pelops's reign and power over the Peloponnese.

After ascending to the throne of Pisa, Pelops married off his sister Niobe to King Amphion of Thebes. This had resulted in a powerful alliance.

Later, he made strategic arrangements for his many children:

His son Alcathous married the daughter of King Magareus of Onchestus and would eventually succeed his father-in-law to the throne.

Pelops' daughter Astydamia married a son of Perseus, Alcaues, the king of Tiryns, and became the mother of Amphitryon.

His daughter Eurydice married King Electryon, the later king of Tiryns and son of Perseus (Through their grand-daughter Alcmene, Pelops and Perseus became great-grandfathers of Heracles).

His son Copreus, who was exiled from Elis, gained favor in the court of his nephew Eurystheus, the king of Mycenae at the time.

His son Atreus, for whom King Tantalus built The Treasury of Atreus, became the king of Mycenae (for a short while and the father of Agamemnon and Menelaus).

His son Hippalcimus became a named Greek hero who was said to have sailed with Jason and the other Argonauts.

PELOPS EXPANDED HIS KINGDOM FROM Pisa to the Isthmus of Corinth. He also carried out various good deeds including building temples and improving infrastructure to better the lives of the people of the Peloponnese.

These good deeds were also intended to make amends with the gods for killing Oenomaus and Myrtilus.

The first known chariot race took place during *The Funeral Games* organized by Pelops to thank the gods for his victory over Oenomaus. An image of that race had been engraved in marble on the pediment of the temple of Zeus in Olympia.

This event marked the founding of "the first Olympic Games."

Hippodamia had also created a contest at Olympia to commemorate her husband's victory. She named it *The Heraea*, in honor of the Olympian Queen goddess Hera.

The event was a footrace for girls. Not much is known about the Heraea and most of our knowledge today comes from Pausanias' description of Greece.

In his description, Pausanias included that the games were considered ancient during his time.

In one of his stories, Pausanias associated sixteen women responsible for the Heraea Foot Race to the conflict between Elis and Pisa following the death of the tyrant Damophon who lived in the sixth century BC. However, most likely, it was reorganized around this time as was the case with other late archaic period events and festivals.

Logically the first chariot races and foot races took place in the fourteenth century BC, Maria summoned. For Pelops lived around the same time as Perseus who fortified had fortified Mycenae at around 1350 BC.

A SHRINE WAS BUILT IN PELOPS' honor at ancient Olympia by Hercules. It had been in existence for a long time, making it widely recognized and accepted.

PELOPS WAS REVERED AS A GOD long before the classical period, when the Olympic games had been established by his cult.

Was the revived Pelops was a giant? Perhaps Hercules was also giant like? Maria speculated, for that would explain the great strength of Hercules.

During the classical period, the Olympic Games were considered the most significant unifying event for all Hellenes.

Athletes from any Greek city-state and kingdom, including Greek colonies outside of Greece, were permitted to travel to ancient Olympia and participate in the Olympic games.

In her research Maria found that evidence of Pelops'

cult activity was present in ancient Olympia since the tenth century, and that cults of Zeus and Hera had predated the first temple of Hera, built around 600 BC.

THE OPENING EVENT OF THE OLYMPIC games had been a spectacular chariot race held at *The Hippodrome of Olympia*, to honor the legendary King Pelops.

The race consisted of forty chariots, each drawn by four horses, and officially began in the seventh century BC.

The race included twelve double laps where several chariots would collide resulting in clouds of dust.

It was a grueling race, with wheels flying off their axles and drivers being tossed in the air, and many contestants never finishing the race.

According to Pausanias, "*The Hippodrome of Olympia was found just south of the Stadium and covered a large area about 600 meters long and 200 meters wide. A wide, flat, open space where the starting point and the finish line were designated with a pole and a second smaller pole called 'Nyssa' designated the turning point.*"

THE PELOPION, THE ALLEGED TOMB of Pelops, was said to be found within the sanctuary of Olympia. It had been enclosed by a circle of stones, within which trees grew and statues were dedicated, located far enough from the temple of Zeus not to intervene with other statues and offerings.

The entrance to the precinct of Pelops was found in the west of the stadium, while the alter to Zeus was approached from and located on the east the stadium.

Maria conducted a thorough search of ancient texts but could not find any mention of Pelops's death. However, she did find that according to Pausanias, *"when Pelops died, his remains were kept in a chest near the sanctuary of Artemis Kordax located near Pisa."*

She searched for the location of the sanctuary of Artemis Kordax and found it in the village of Elis.

According to Pausanias: *"One sees traces of a sanctuary of Artemis, surnamed Kordax [at Pisa in Elis] because the followers of Pelops celebrated their victory by the side of this goddess and danced the cordax, a dance peculiar to the dwellers round Mount Sipylos [in Lydia]."*

Pelops must have built it, mused Maria.

Upon further research Maria discovered that during the classical period the cordax (κόρδαξ), was a provocative, licentious, and often obscene mask dance of ancient Greek comedy.

Interesting, maybe sarcasm? Maria wondered.

The bones of Pelops continued to be important in ancient Greece for centuries to come, especially the divinely made shoulder bone.

Pausanias included a story of *The Sacred Bone of Pelops*: *"One of the conditions for allowing the victory at Troy was the presence of the bone of Pelops amongst the Greeks. Agamemnon sent a ship to bring the sacred bone from Pisa to Troy. However, the ship and its precious cargo were lost during a storm near the coast of Eretria, a town in Euboea facing the coast of Attica, across the narrow South Euboean Gulf."*

When Maria saw the name Eretria, it looked familiar. After searching, she found that the coastal town still existed today.

That's why, years before, Maria drove through Evia with a friend, and they had made a stop at Eretria.

Eretria meant "city of the rowers," and it had been an important Greek polis during classical times, mentioned by many famous writers.

Many years after the Trojan War, a local fisherman named Demarmenus had found the ivory bone of Pelops tangled in his fishing net.

He didn't know what it was and decided to take it to Delphi to seek guidance.

Coincidentally, at the same time, a committee from Elis was also in Delphi seeking guidance for a plague that had been ravaging their district.

The Pythia brought the two parties together and advised that the sacred bone of Pelops be returned to its homeland.

They followed the advice and returned to Elis, where they placed the sacred bone back in its chest, and soon after, the plague was abated and eventually disappeared.

Demarnenus was honored for his discovery. He would move to Elis where he was assigned the position of "Guardian of the Bone."

Pausanias mentioned that *"at the sanctuary of Olympia, libations were offered to the dark-faced Pelops during night-time rituals before being offered to Zeus the following day."*

He also noted that the magistrates of the year sacrificed a black ram at the precinct of Pelops, and portions of the animal were later distributed among the cult personnel as part of a banquet.

The sanctuary of Ancient Olympia was named after the Olympian gods who resided on Mount Olympus, the highest mountain in Greece, located on the border between Thessaly and Macedonia.

The significance of the Olympic games in connection to the sanctuary was said to have started during *the Proto-Geometric era*, a period of Ancient Greek pottery production that began in Athens around 1030 BC and continued until roughly 900 BC.

Pottery production was the first expression of a reviving civilization after the collapse of Mycenaean culture.

THE OLYMPIAN SANCTUARY, dedicated to Zeus, was located at the confluence of the Alpheios and Kladeos rivers on the banks of the Alpheios river. It was situated in a lush green area at the southwest foot of Mount Kronio.

The Temple of Zeus housed an impressive gold and ivory statue of Zeus seated on a throne.

The statue, which was sculpted by the renowned artist Pheidias, was about 41 feet tall and earned the title: "One of the seven wonders of the ancient world."

According to Pausanias, the temple was 68 feet high up to the pediment, 95 feet wide, and 230 feet long. It was approached by a ramp on the east side.

THE OLYMPIA STADIUM WAS THE largest stadium in the Peloponnese and a significant attraction, along with the temple of Zeus.

During the classical period, the Olympian sanctuary served as a center for athletics and religion, and various buildings were added to it over time.

They included the Gymnasium, which was used for training competitors, the Palaestra, a wrestling school and grounds, the Leonidaion, a guest house designed and donated by Leonidas of Naxos, and public baths.

In the fourth century BC, King Philip II built the Philippeion, an elegant Ionic Tholos that was used to host statues dedicated by the Macedonians.

The spaces between buildings were filled with a variety of votive offerings, including statues and tripods.

THE SANCTUARY OF ANCIENT Olympia began to lose its charm during late Hellenistic times.

Although the Romans added several new buildings and structures during their administration in the following centuries, the games were not fully revived.

The last recorded games were held under Theodosius I in 393 BC, but archaeological evidence suggested that some games were still being held after that time.

In 86 BC the Roman general Sulla badly plundered the sanctuary.

A new wave of construction took place in the second century AD, funded by Herodes Atticus, who built an aqueduct at the sanctuary.

Because the threat of barbarians had persisted, Herodes had erected a defensive wall around the temple of Zeus and the Bouleuterion.

The Bouleuterion had been built at the height of the Olympic games, in the sixth century BC, for local legislatures and other meetings. It was an assembly house comprising two main buildings, a square room, and a stoa.

Herodes Atticus, along with his wife Appia Annia Regilla, had built a beautiful nymphaeum, dedicated to *The Nymphs of the Springs.*

CHAPTER 15

Herodes Atticus was an Athenian rhetorician and a Roman senator. Born into Athenian royalty he had claimed lineage from several mythic Greek kings. They had included Theseus, Cecrops, and Aeacus, as well as Zeus.

His wife, Appia Annia Regilla, was a wealthy and influential Roman aristocrat with family relations and ties to many Roman emperors and empresses.

Herodes Atticus had received the best education that money could buy. After completing a course of honors in civil posts, he had demonstrated his talent for civil engineering, particularly in the design and construction of water-supply systems.

He also had a passion for philosophy and rhetoric and was widely known for his literary works, although unfortunately most of them have been lost over time.

Herodes was an important writer and scholar, and a public benefactor on an imperial scale, not just in Athens but also in other parts of Greece and Asia Minor.

He held many important posts, was a friend and kinsman of emperors, and was widely respected for his contributions to society.

During his reign, Herodes of Athens sponsored various public works, many of which still exist today.

He also funded numerous building projects with the most notable being: *The Panathenaic Stadium—Athens, the Odeon of Herodes Atticus—Athens, a theater at Corinth, a stadium at Delphi, the baths at Thermopylae, an aqueduct at Canusium in Italy, an aqueduct at Alexandria Troas, and the Nymphaeum at Olympia.*

The Odeon of Herodes Atticus was his most famous project.

A stone Roman theater structure situated on the southwest slope of the Acropolis, built in honor of his Roman wife.

The theatre, which had a capacity for 5,000 people, had a steep-sloped design, with a three-story stone front wall and a wooden roof made of expensive cedar of Lebanese timber.

Unfortunately, the theatre was destroyed and left in ruins by the Heruli, an ancient Germanic tribe, in 267 AD.

However, it was later renovated in 1950 and was now extensively used, mostly for music concerts and ancient plays.

Herodes was also famously known for another structure which was located near the east coast of the Peloponnese, not far from where Maria lived.

The impressive *Villa of Herodes Atticus* was found at the ancient town of Eva.

The villa spanned an enormous ground area of 20,000 square meters, making it "the largest known villa in all of Greece."

It was built in the Roman architectural style and had included a mansion, an atrium with galleries, a bath complex, and a sanctuary.

The location of the villa was known since 1805 when the English traveler William Martin Leake pointed it out and mentioned its ruins in his writings.

However, it had been the German archaeologist, historian, and museum director, Ernst Gurtius, who visited the area in the mid-nineteenth century and noted that "the ruins belonged to a grand villa and not some settlement as previously thought."

According to the monks of the adjacent Loukou Monastery, archaeological finds were already abundant in the area before the nineteenth century. They claimed to have continuously discovered antiquities while cultivating the surrounding land.

In 1980, excavations of the area revealed spectacular findings, including mosaics, inscriptions, statues, and other works of art.

The archaeological finds had confirmed stories that had been told since ancient times, describing this villa as "more like a museum."

MARIA CONDUCTED SOME ADDITIONAL research and found that the villa was partially destroyed towards the end of the fourth century, possibly due to an earthquake or as a result of Visigoth invasions. And that, in the early fifth century, the baths and other sections of the villa were dismantled and used for craft production.

She also discovered that the northern wing of the villa was later modified to create a large basilica, however this structure fell apart a few centuries later, presumably following a major earthquake in 856 AD.

SOME OF THE RUINS OF the villa were said to be found at the nearby grounds of *The Loukou Monastery.*

The monastery dated back to the twelfth century, and was located 250 meters south of the villa, on the opposite side of the road.

It was said to have housed many ancient artifacts of which some had been incorporated into the masonry of the historic church, nunnery, and surrounding walls.

DURING ANCIENT TIMES, the town of Eva was considered one of the most significant towns on the outskirts of ancient Thyrea.

The town's ancient name, Eva, had been confirmed by current archaeological findings in the area.

Pausanias had mentioned Eva as still existing as a village during his visit.

MARIA MANAGED TO FIND SOME additional information on ancient Eva in a section of *The Dictionary of Greek and Roman Geography (1854) by William Smith, LLD, Ed.*:

"Besides Thyrea and Anthena or Athena [Anthini], mentioned by Thucydides, two other places in the Thyreatis are noticed by Pausanias, namely, NERIS (Νηρίς) and EVA (Εὔα). Pausanias entered the Thyreatis by the pass of the Anigraea; and after following the road along the coast, turned upwards into the interior, and came to Thyrea (ἰόντι ἄνω πρὸς τὴν ἤπειρον Θυρέα χωρίον ἐστίν), where he saw the sepulchers of the 300 Argive, and 300 Spartan champions. On leaving these, he came first to Anthena, next to Neris, and lastly to Eva, which he describes as the largest of the three villages, containing a sanctuary of Polemocrates, son of Machaon, who was honored here as a god or hero of the healing art. Above these villages was the range of Mt. Parnon, where, not far from the sources of the Tanus, the boundaries of the Lacedaemonians, Argives, and Tegeatae joined, and were marked by stone Hermae."

Maria focused on the section: *"On leaving these, he came first to Anthena, next to Neris, and lastly to Eva, which he describes as the largest of the three villages, containing a sanctuary of Polemocrates, son of Machaon, who was honored here as a god or hero of the healing art."*

But why wasn't The Villa of Herodes Atticus mentioned? This had puzzled Maria. She searched again and confirmed that Pausanias had indeed made no mention of the massive villa.

This was an odd omission, considering that Herodes had lived around the same time as Pausanias. In fact, Herodes died in 177 AD, at the age of 76, while Pausanias had died in 180 AD, at the age of 70, which made Pausanias a few years younger and increased the likelihood of the villa either being built or standing at the time of his visit.

Maria had heard local stories about Herodes choosing to build his villa in the ancient town of Eva due to its dry climate. Even today, as she drove through the town, Maria noticed that the air was much dryer and the climate more comfortable in the area.

The ancients knew about the negative effects of humidity.

Herodes was not the only one who built in ancient Eva, for over a thousand years before him, the great healer and doctor Polemocrates had built his sanctuary in the same area.

And later, most likely during the classical period, a temple had also been built there, in his honor.

Polemocrates was the grandson of the famous doctor and healer Asclepius, whose sanctuary and temple were also found on the Peloponnese, at the site of ancient Epidaurus in the Argolis region.

It was strongly believed that the grounds where the monastery now stood were the same grounds where the ancient sanctuary of Polemocrates had also stood—over three thousand years before.

Interesting, there must be a greater connection between the three. Maria was intrigued by the potential connection between the ancient temple, the villa, and the monastery.

She had a hunch that there was more to it than met the eye.

To investigate further, Maria decided to drive to the Eva region, which was just a short distance away.

Upon arriving, she discovered that the monastery was situated on a small hill directly across from the villa ruins. And although the villa ruins were fenced in and inaccessible, the monastery was open and accessible.

She turned left toward the monastery grounds.

As Maria was driving up to the monastery, she stopped to admire an impressive two-arch structure on her left.

It looked like a natural bridge that blended seamlessly with its surroundings, she pulled out her mobile phone to research it and discovered that it was actually an ancient aqueduct built during the Roman era.

Wow, who would have thought . . . Not only that, for it was believed to be the oldest still-standing aqueduct in all of Europe!"

As she drove up the road that led to the parking area near the gate, she couldn't help but notice that the tall, whitewashed outer walls and the windows of the nuns' quarters gave the monastery the appearance of a fortress.

When she got to the parking lot and stepped out of her car Maria immediately felt a sense of calm.

After passing the gate she found that within the walls there was a beautiful, paved courtyard, filled with flowers, palms and a variety of fruit trees.

Maria walked around alone for a few moments, taking in the garden, which felt almost like the grounds of an archaeological museum, as it was surrounded by relics of antiquity.

Broken column bases and capitals, along with other marble decorative pieces and architectural elements such as parapets, were scattered throughout. There were even a few statues.

Maria then took notice of some intact column bases lined up in a circle.

They must have been part of a round ancient structure. Perhaps a healing temple! Maria was getting excited.

As she gazed at the exterior of the church, she noticed that fragments of old marble and other decorative elements had been integrated into the walls.

"*How fascinating!*" To her surprise, right next to the church, a rather large ancient statue of the goddess Eva still stood under a stone arch.

After a few minutes, a nun came out of the convent in order to open the church door for Maria.

Maria walked toward her.

The nun, who was rather young, had a radiant face and a smile that seemed to reflect the peaceful and healing energy of the place that Maria was also feeling.

"Hi, I have taken some pictures of the grounds, hope that's okay?" asked Maria.

"That is fine, but no pictures are allowed inside the church," the nun responded.

Maria added "Are you from around here?"

"No," the nun smiled again and walked to the door of the church. Maria followed.

Upon entering, Maria quickly scanned the interior to

confirm that additional ancient archaeological pieces had been integrated into the walls.

She also noticed that the floor was composed of different colored marble sections.

Next, she headed over to the slot and inserted a two-euro coin, then she picked up three small candles and lit them for the well-being of her two children and herself.

EXITING THE CHURCH, MARIA NOT only expressed her gratitude towards the young nun, but she also shared her thoughts regarding the ancient pieces found on the monastery grounds.

"How about if the ancient pieces found on the grounds actually came from the monastery grounds instead of the villa nearby?" Which was what the nun had claimed.

The nun was surprised by Maria's observation. Her mouth dropped open.

However, Maria didn't say anything more. She just smiled at the nun before turning and walking towards the parking lot.

Yes, it must have been the other way around. Maria was sure of it.

THE LOUKOU MONASTERY WAS considered to be the most easily accessible monastery in all of Arcadia and said to be "one of the most picturesque monasteries of the whole of the Peloponnese."

The name of the Loukou monastery came from the Latin word Lucus, meaning "sacred grove."

Historical records and archaeological evidence revealed that the monastery was home to an early Christian church that dated back to the fifth century AD.

The church was originally built in *the catholicon style* and decorated with fine wall paintings. However, at some point, the interior of the church had been re-built to confirm with the Orthodox church structure.

That explained the patches of different styled and colored floor marble. There must have been walls, separations and other structures which were removed, Maria mused.

The monastery's library boasted a collection of 300 volumes of manuscripts, patriarch sigils, codices, and numerous other relics.

POLEMOCRATES WAS SAID to have been a highly skilled ancient Greek physician, which must have been the case, given that he was the grandson of the famous ancient healer, Asclepius.

And although not much information is available about Polemocrates, it was known that he had a sanctuary in the village of Eva *"where he was worshipped as a god or hero of the healing arts."*

ASCLEPIUS, SAID TO BE THE SON of Apollo, was considered a hero and "the god of medicine."

He represented the healing aspect of medicine, and his physicians and attendants were known as the *Therapeutae of Asclepius.*

The rod of Asclepius, a snake-entwined staff, remained to be the symbol of medicine, and *the Hippocratic Oath by*

Apollo, taken by medical professionals, was based on the principles taught by Asclepius.

It was known that Asclepius and his grandson were both healers and doctors who practiced their craft at the Epidaurus and Eva sanctuaries and when they retired, their students and subsequent generations continued their legacy by establishing their own sanctuaries at different locations.

IN ANCIENT TIMES, IT WAS customary to bring large gifts of gratitude, such as statues, to temples, similar to the offerings brought to the oracles at Delphi for advice.

This tradition still continued in modern-day Greece, where people give small gold or silver gifts to churches and monasteries as a way of showing gratitude for healing.

These gifts often depicted the specific part of the body that was healed and were hung inside the churches, often near the healing icon.

MARIA TOOK A BREAK. SHE WAS done researching for the day. However, later that evening, while scrolling social media, Maria came across a post that contained an image and information about the marble head of the goddess Hygeia which had recently been uncovered.

Hygeia was the daughter of Asclepius and the goddess of health.

The marble head had been discovered in a healing sanctuary dedicated to Asclepius in Feneos Peloponnese.

Maria searched for Feneos and found that it was an archaeological site located in northern Peloponnese, between Corinth and Patra.

She realized that the marble head's date, fifth to sixth century BC, coincided with the height of the Olympic games.

Wouldn't visitors need places to stay and rest along the way? Also, theaters for entertainment? And wouldn't it make perfect sense for them to also visit healing sanctuaries?

This would logically hold true not only for visitors, but also for athletes before and/or after competing in events.

Especially the healing temples, Maria noted.

Now pieces were starting to fit together perfectly, just like getting to the end of a jigsaw puzzle.

WE DON'T KNOW MUCH ABOUT Polemocrates temple however we do know about his grandfathers. And, they were probably very similar, Maria surmised.

Let's see what that was like. She searched and found the following:

- *In a small valley in the Peloponnesus, the shrine of Asclepios, the god of medicine, developed out of a much earlier cult of Apollo (Maleates), during the 6th century BC at the latest, as the official cult of the city state of Epidaurus.*
- *Its principal monuments, particularly the temple of Asclepios, the Tholos, and the Theatre—considered one of the purest masterpieces of Greek architecture—date from the 4th century.*
- *The vast site, with its temples and hospital buildings devoted to its healing gods, provides valuable insight into the healing cults of Greek and Roman times.*
- *The Sanctuary is the earliest organized sanatorium and is significant for its association with the history*

of medicine, providing evidence of the transition from belief in divine healing to the science of medicine.

- *Among the facilities of the classical period are buildings that represent all the functions of the Sanctuary, including healing cults and rituals, library, baths, sports, accommodation, hospital, and theatre.*

If the sanctuary of Polemocrates was anything like that of his grandfather, it would have consisted of similar structures and covered a large area. Possibly an area that included the grounds of both the monastery and villa, Maria surmised.

MARIA SEARCHED UNDER Polemocrates again. This time for his family history.

She found that his father Machaon along with his younger brother Podaliriushis, "had led an army from Tricca (today's Trikala of Thessaly) in the Trojan War, fighting alongside the Greeks."

Since the Trojan War dated to 1250 BC, Polemocrates must have lived in the thirteen century BC. And since this was the only sanctuary that had been mentioned in ancient writings, that meant that after studying with his grandfather, Polemocrates moved to ancient Eva to start his own practice.

"So, some of the ancient ruins and artifacts found at the ancient Eva sites must date back to that period!" Maria was now getting excited.

HMM . . . AND HERODES' Villa was built just across . . . What if the huge villa, that was more like a museum, had not been the only structure built there?

Perhaps during the classical period, at the height of the Olympic games, there were buildings found there, for the different functions of "Polemocrates Sanctuary," just as his grandfather's.

Then Maria got the goosepimples. This usually happened to her when she was on to something "big."

What if Herodes built the huge villa on the site to protect the ancient architecture and finds of the sanctuary? After all, isn't that what he had attempted to do at Olympia, protect and attempt to rebuild the ancient site?

"*Of course!*" she exclaimed.

By making it his private property and having guards around to protect the villa grounds … by effectively "owning the ancient site," he succeeded at ancient Eva what he had failed to do at ancient Olympia—the effective protection of ancient architecture, sculptures, and other arts from looting and destruction!

"*Μπράβο του!*" *Smart move. Very smart move . . .*

And Pausanias's writings did not include the magnificent villa for the same reason.

It all made perfect sense now.

CHAPTER 16

In her search on Herodes Villa at ancient Eva, Maria managed to find a fine detailed report regarding its history, features, and archeological finds:

Appropriation and Synthesis report of the Villa of Herodes Atticus at Eva (Loukou), Greece—by George Spyropoulos (Head of the Department of Prehistoric and Classical Antiquities and the Department of Museums of the Ephorate of Antiquities of Corinth, Deputy Director of the Ephorate of Antiquities of Corinth):

A syncretic blending of Egyptian, Greek, and Roman features can be found in varying degrees in Roman villas throughout the empire, including at the Villa Farnesina and the House of Augustus in Rome, Hadrian's Villa in Tivoli, and the villa of Herodes Atticus (AD 103– 177), the noted Greek intellectual and cultural leader of Athenian ancestry, in Eva (Loukou), Greece.

Recent scholarship recognizes that the cultural mixing of what could be considered typical Greek or Roman motifs with decorative Egyptianizing motifs "serve[d] as a stylistic reflection of an appropriation of . . . conquered cultures by means of integration" into a new imperial visual language.1 This paper will argue that what Jennifer Trimble described as "a sophisticated and imperializing Augustan engagement with pharaonic visual culture," referring specifically to the Ara Pacis Augustae in light of the Egyptianizing of Rome's urban landscape achieved by the two obelisks Augustus brought from Egypt to Rome, continued under Hadrian and is found in the splendid but subtle decorative elements in Herodes Atticus's villa.

Before excavation the villa of Herodes Atticus at Eva (Loukou) rose as a mound amid the hollows and ravines of the site. A kiln in operation from around 1950 had burned many ancient finds for lime, and innumerable marble chips covered the uncultivated area in heaps. The entire area was expropriated and secured and plowing and the cultivation of olive trees were prohibited in order to protect the villa from further damage. In 1979 systematic excavation began under the supervision of Theodore Spyropoulos.

Many parts of the villa were covered by thick bushes, the roots of which had grown deep into the ancient remains and caused, in some cases, serious damage to the mosaic pavements. As was reported by the excavator, modern agricultural activity and the exploitation of the arable strips of land around the villa had moved several antiquities as far as hundreds of meters to the north and to the south. Some portrait heads, now in the

Archaeological Museum of Astros, were found mutilated by plowing on the lower level to the north of the villa.

The villa is arranged on three levels. The first part to be excavated was the monumental staircase that leads to the entrance of the Great Hall toward the northern end of the villa. The steps of the staircase are now covered by tiles but were originally riveted with schist plaques, fragments of which have been found either in situ or around the base of the staircase. The staircase leads somewhat steeply to the north, having as its starting point the mosaic pavements that form the surface of the villa's upper level.

First Level of the Villa

The first level was deeper than the others due to natural land formation and was adapted to accept the heavy construction of a large hypostyle hall (Great Northern Basilica), a typical hypostylos aethousa with two rows of internal colonnades supporting the roof. The walls of the hall were constructed from rectangular ashlar blocks interrupted at regular intervals by courses of strips of flat bricks. Externally these were covered by a thick layer of plaster to which marble panels were attached, some of which are still in situ. The entrance to the hall contains a large marble lintel, its sides decorated with semicolumns. Stratigraphically the various parts of the monument present a divergent picture. The thick layer of debris of the destruction level, which covers the ruins, consists of reddish soil filled with small stones, tiles, and fragments of schist and marble slabs, as well as bricks and plaster from the walls, including the mural decorations and the pavements of the villa. Inside the Great Hall this layer measures up to 3.5 meters high, a huge mass of rubble, which was kept in place thanks to the preservation of the strong walls of the building. This layer has not been removed since it fell and covered the hall, which occurred after it was found plundered and ransacked. The columns and the capitals were found at different levels of the layer of destruction, testifying to a gradual collapse of the deserted villa. Vandalism should not be excluded as the first and main destructive agent, and this might reasonably be attributed to the invasion of the Visigoths in the Peloponnese at the end of the fourth century AD.

The axiality of the basilica was enhanced by the addition of an apse on the west side with five niches for statuary and columns of Cipollino marble projecting between them. The surface of the mass of the walls was enlivened by reflected light and shadow in much the same style as the illusions of recesses and projections in the wall paintings of the villa of P. Fannius Synistor at Boscoreale, "an exceptional example of late Second Style decoration, teasing the eye with perspectival recession" and encouraging viewers to look above the barrier of the socle "and out into fantastic panoramas or architectural confections."10 The columns of the main core of the basilica are also unfluted monoliths of gray-green Cipollino marble. The capitals, which are composite, are of Pentelic marble and date from the Flavian period, while those of the apse are Hadrianic. Building work on the basilica seems therefore to have been carried out in two phases. The first phase provided Herodes with the main core of the basilica, built by his father, Tiberius Claudius Atticus, or even his grandfather Hipparchus, who might have purchased the land when the family fled

*to Sparta after Hipparchus had been accused of tyranny.
In the second phase, during the lifetime of Herodes, the
initial plan of the basilica was expanded by the addition
of the apse on the west side, a palaestra on the east, and
a turris (observation tower) on the northeast, while at
the same time construction of the villa was nearing completion. The eastern part of the great hypostyle hall was
transformed into a basilica during the early Christian
era judging by the closing of the two narrower arched
entrances at the east wall and the thick layer of lime
on the inside of the same wall, on which two illegible
inscriptions of this period were traced.*

*Among the sculptural decorations of the basilica is a
colossal statue of Athena placed in one of the niches of the
apse.11 Also discovered there were portraits of Herodes
and his family,12 grave reliefs, and an inscribed stela
of the Erechtheis tribe with the names of those who died
at the Battle of Marathon, a monument to the heroized
dead from the grave of the Athenians at Marathon. It
is probably because of the importance of the battle to the
Athenians that Herodes Atticus decided to integrate the
stela into his villa, in accordance with the funerary tone
and memorializing aspects of the site.*

Second, Upper Level of the Villa

*The second, upper level includes a garden terrace (bel-
vedere), well defined by two walls running from east
to west and overlooking the Argolic Gulf. Moving to
the west, next to the garden terrace is a structure with a
hairpin-shaped plan, identified as the Garden-Stadion
of the villa, comprising two nymphaea on the west side
and two symmetrical rooms, while in the middle there*

*was a court on a higher level, which served as a triclin-
ium (large dining hall). The most important sculptures
found in the Garden-Stadion are those belonging to the
Dionysian thiasos—a statue of Dionysos, a statuette of
Pan, and others—which clearly indicate that, as with
Hadrian's Villa, some parts of the villa evoked a bucolic
landscape peopled with Dionysian figures that sym-
bolized a carefree life.14 Two statues of Herakles were
conceived as pendants, displayed as a symmetrical pair.
A left hand of the hero holding the apples of the Hesperides was found, showing that the statue was probably
a copy of the so-called Farnese Herakles, attributed to the
fourth-century BC sculptor Lysippos. A headless statue
holding the lion skin in his left hand and most probably
a club in his now missing right hand is similar in both
style and execution to the so-called Lansdowne Herakles,
a Hadrianic copy of an original of the fourth century BC,
clearly associated with the style of Skopas, currently on
display at the Getty Villa in Los Angeles.*

*On the same level, west of the Garden-Stadion and
above the Great Northern Basilica, is the heart of the
villa: the atrium and an open garden—skillfully adapted
to the landscape—surrounded by a rectangular peristyle
running from east to west. The second and main cluster
of buildings was accommodated by an extensive arti-
ficial terrace. As William L. MacDonald has correctly
remarked: "Of course making a terrace meant making
level ground, but leveling alone would not produce one.
A terrace must be elevated, its platform a level stretch,
set well above an area or vista, whose existence was
part of the terrace's definition. Terrace building, a prime
Roman occupation, invited the incorporated construction*

of cryptoportici, simultaneously lessening the amount of fill required and providing useful space." Cryptoportici have not been found at Eva, although one probably lies under the floor of the south stoa. This upper part of the villa has suffered severely from the effects of cultivation, and its upper part was completely erased and planted with olive trees. Some trial trenches opened there have indicated that the space was plowed and cleaned, and everything was removed and dispersed or embedded in modern retaining walls around the area.

The admirable adaptation of the residential and other buildings of the villa into the landscape of the site of Eva is apparent, a practice that has a long tradition in the Hellenistic world starting with Pergamon. It continued with the Delian house plans, framed in the Hellenistic urban architecture known also from Pella, Vergina, and elsewhere and followed by the aristocratic inhabitants of Pompeii and the cities of the Greco-Roman world. Planning was impacted by the topographic requirements of the site, but certain features are typical. There is usually a peristyle court with colonnades on all four sides, one of them sometimes equipped with an upper gallery (the so-called Rhodian portico). There is always a cistern beneath the court as well as mosaic pavements in the court, the passages, and the entrance lobbies and formal reception rooms that opened onto the colonnade. From the middle of the first century AD, Roman villas of wealthy citizens presented an internal court framed by colonnades on three sides only, judging by villas in Campania, Apulia, and Rome itself.18 Two basic architectural types emerged, both with origins in the East. The peristyle villas, direct descendants of Hellenistic palaces, are frequently reflected in Campanian wall paintings, though the porticus villas, according to Karl Swoboda, evolved from a long, narrow row of rooms opening onto a road or court.

The planning of the villa of Herodes Atticus at Eva was in accordance with the architectural tradition of the Hellenistic metropolis and its survival or circumstantial alterations, which were introduced to suit the taste and the needs of the Roman aristocracy. From this point of view, Herodes Atticus is shown to be a citizen of two worlds and an heir of two cultural traditions, a fact that is underlined by the mosaic pavements as well as the sculptural groups discussed below. The villa of Herodes Atticus at Eva is, properly speaking, a villa maritima, lying about five kilometers from the coastal site of Thyrea. As Alexander McKay remarks, "Coastal estates were eagerly sought after with the advent of Hellenistic luxury to Italy after the wars of conquest abroad." Such villas gradually became "the paradigm of luxury and a habitual topic for moralists and poets."

To imagine what the villa was like at the time of Herodes Atticus requires the reconstruction of the surviving elements. One may reasonably suppose that it was surrounded by a brick-built wall faced in marble and fronted by a fine peristyle. The floor consisted of a mosaic pavement, like the peridromos outside it. All around the peristyle a deep channel measuring 170 meters in length was constructed. First, a wide trench was cut in the native soil. The trench was smoothed externally and then covered by a retaining wall made of baked bricks, which were in turn plastered and painted red and blue. The pavement of the trench was also riveted with large orthogonal bricks, also plastered and painted. This arti-ficial pool—an ingenious impluvium—was filled with water to create an allusion to a Nilotic setting, like the channels in Hadrian's Villa at Tivoli.21 An aqueduct brought water from a local spring in the mountains. Remains of this construction are still visible, comprising walls and columns and an intact bridge of the Roman imperial period. It is exactly there in the hollow ditch that most of the villa's remarkable sculptures were found. The ditch was filled with rubble and soil, bricks, tiles, bases, columns, and capitals, as well as sculptures either from the atrium or from the peridromos and the stoas that run all around it. The filling of the ditch eluci-dates some details of the fortunes of the villa. In its upper layers, it contains brown soil, pebbles, and small stones from the arable estates, fragments of bricks and tiles from the atrium and the stoa, and chips and fragments of marble and schist slabs and even of sculpture. The debris below contained columns, capitals, fragments of statues, marble reliefs, and some pottery fragments of lamps of the Roman imperial and early Christian periods.

Three sides of the atrium were expanded to stoas decorated with mosaic pavements. The mosaics of the villa testify to excellent skill in their execution and to a high artistic standard in their conception and composition. One can see here the devices of foreshortening and chiaroscuro and the three-dimensional quality of the famous compositions at Delos, Pompeii, and Sparta. The mosaics at Eva are highly decorative, enlivened in many cases by small rectangular panels representing women, most of them muses or nymphs, shown as either busts or figures in conventional gestures and poses, such *as the nymph Arethusa, from the southern part of the peridromos. Their voluminous upper bodies resemble statues of the second century AD (like the Tragoedia from Pergamon), and their faces are rendered in a classicizing, eclectic style. The rich and densely woven geometric patterns are skillfully executed and endlessly repeated in a continuous, tapestry-like surface, which undeniably imitated the carpets that covered the corridors of the houses from Hellenistic Delos to Greco-Roman Pompeii and Sparta. Yet this continuity is only the result of the skillful juxtaposition of larger squares decorated with exactly the same repertory. They are impressive and enhance the effect of luxury and delicacy of the decorative components of the rich villa.*

This impressive and thick peristyle enhanced the symmetry of the atrium and the ditch and opened the scenery to the stoas behind it. The columns of the stoas were, as in the Great Northern Basilica, of unfluted Cipollino marble with Corinthian capitals of white Pentelic marble like those of the main core of the basilica, which were fluted and elegantly carved with abundant use of a drill. The rear wall of the stoas has been only partly preserved. It was made of small stones, and its inner face was thickly plastered and then riveted with marble slabs, some of which were preserved in situ. The roof inclined inward and reached the edge of the ditch where the rain fell in. Many large fragments of roof tiles were uncovered in the relevant places. As to the shape of the stoas, some relics suggest a low wall base in the middle to bridge their relatively large depth. The rear walls were undeniably the place where the fine reliefs found in the excavation were attached. The west side of the atrium was occupied by a nymphaeum and an exedra erected upon it, an architectural construction ingeniously adapted to the setting of the villa's main compartments, which can be restored as having a facade of rows of niches decorated with portraits of Herodes Atticus, his friends and companions, and the imperial family. Portraits include those of Hadrian, Septimius Severus, Marcus Aurelius, Commodus, Publius Vedius Antoninus, an unknown man dressed in a Greek mantle, an unknown woman (probably Elpiniki, daughter of Herodes Atticus), and Herodes Atticus himself. In the villa of Herodes Atticus, the portraits displayed in the exedra and the atrium were meant to act as companions for the visitors, recalling the memory of the dead. Some are posthumous commemorations of his wife, children, and adopted students, who all died very young, but it was a commemoration that had the primary purpose of placing an emphasis on Herodes Atticus himself.

Bust of Emperor Hadrian. The usual image of the mythical gorgon Medusa decorating the emperor's breast-plate has been replaced by a portrait of Antinous. The bust was found on the western side of the river, close to the exedra on which it stood, along with many other portraits.

Below the portraits, the front side of the nymphaeum is pierced with six niches in which six statues of young girls in windblown drapery were originally placed. The young girls, of which one is almost fully preserved, have been identified as the Dancing Caryatids by the sculptor Kallimachos, a work of the last decade of the fifth century BC. Opposite and in exact correspondence with the Dancing Caryatids stood, instead of columns, six caryatids supporting the roof of the east stoa of the atrium, overlooking the river, and seven columns behind the caryatids, thus creating a small pavilion. It is hard not to see here the influence of Herodes Atticus himself and his close involvement in the architectural genesis of the site, which, as Trimble writes of the Ara Pacis, "is understood to embody multi-layered appropriations of the past, recombined in sophisticated and innovative ways to meet the needs of the present."26 Everything indicates his propensity for assigning complex meanings to architectural forms and associating himself with the cosmos. Cosmic imagery was particularly popular in Roman architecture, as seen at the Pantheon in Rome and in Hadrian's sprawling residence at Tivoli. Nowhere was there a better opportunity for cosmic expression than in imperial, and especially residential, architecture. One of the buildings at Hadrian's villa—known as the Teatro Marittimo, or Island Enclosure—is very similar to one at the villa of Herodes Atticus. It consists of a colonnaded portico, within which is a circular canal with an island at its center.28 As far as the rest of the sculptural decoration of the main core of the villa is concerned, it should be noted that another statue of Dionysos indicates that this part of the villa, like the Garden–Stadion, also resembled a bucolic landscape inhabited by Dionysian figures. Portrait galleries abounded, statues of athletes evoked a Greek gymnasium, and decorative landscape and votive reliefs were attached to the rear walls of the three stoas.

At the north and south stoas of the villa, respectively, stood the famous Hellenistic sculptural groups: the Pasquino (Menelaus holding the body of Patroclus) and the group of Achilles with Penthesilea, with whom he fell in love after having mortally wounded her. Both are Roman copies of lost originals of the Hellenistic age. The Achilles and Penthesilea group has been found and reconstructed, but the Pasquino is lost. The discovery, however, of two mosaic pavements from the south and north stoas representing the groups prove that the Pasquino once stood there.

To the west, the border of the villa is designated by a large hall with an apse on the west side and five niches for statuary. This building has been identified as the Western Basilica. The two suites of rooms to the north and south of the basilica are likely sacella or lararia, since dedicatory inscriptions, as well as portraits, of a type often placed in lararia were discovered there. One of the side rooms of the basilica must have served as a sanctuary of Isis, judging by the discovery of the head and bust of Artemis Ephesia and the portrait of a youth whose hairstyle is associated with followers of Isis.

Bust of Artemis Ephesia. This bust represents a copy of the cult statue of Artemis, known mainly from coins. On her head she wears a polos decorated with rosettes, sphinxes, and deer, one of her companion animals. From the sides of the polos emerges a disc decorated with a star on the proper right side. The upper part of her breastplate is decorated with a necklace, from which acorns hang. The lower part of her breast supports, up to its point of preservation, two rows of breasts as a fertility symbol or, as other scholars have suggested, gourds, also a fertility symbol.

The third level of the villa contains some very interesting installations. Starting from east to west and along the main axis, one encounters the Temple-Sanctuary of

Truly it was more of a museum. Maria was awed by the
report and its findings and wondered where the art and
other pieces unearthed were stored today.

CHAPTER 17

Maria once shared with her archeologist niece, "If I had it to do over again, I would become an archeologist. There is so much that is still undiscovered."

Her niece had responded, "Hopefully, we will leave something for future generations to find."

This made Maria realize that if every hidden secret of Peloponnese antiquity had already been uncovered, both current and future generations of archaeologists would be left with nothing to discover and would become very bored.

And although she understood the laid-back attitude of her niece and the general Greek mindset, she could not operate with the same approach.

For Maria, it was essential to analyze everything, establish connections, and arrive at a conclusion.

This was simply how her brain functioned.

Then she remembered something a friend in Southern California, who had left Greece to live and work in the United States, had said to her: "It is a choice, it is who we are, we need to be challenged and move further forward."

Yes indeed, Maria now understood.

ONE AFTERNOON, AS MARIA WAS returning home after taking some items to the supply room of the village house, she stopped by the site of Herodes' Villa.

Although the site was fenced in and inaccessible, she walked around it to get a sense of the area.

That's when Maria realized the villa also had an unobstructed view of the sea and the coast of the Argolic Gulf. The view continued all the way across to Nafplion.

Having a view of nature was important to Maria. Even though Maria's village house did not have a sea view, it had an unobstructed view of the valley and the mountain ranges beyond, as far as the eye could see.

Her plans were to move into the house in the village once the upstairs was finished. The downstairs would be built at a later date, to be used by guests and Maria's children whenever they decided to visit.

Before building the downstairs, she would build a swimming pool in the side yard, in order to get her exercise and also enjoy with visitors.

The swimming pool would also later serve as an incentive for family and friends to visit and stay longer.

Thankfully, the house stood on a ten-thousand-square-foot lot, providing ample space for Maria to carry out her plans.

The lot comprised a front patio downstairs, a side yard, and a large area at the back filled with olive trees.

At the back side of the house, she planned to construct a spacious veranda, which will be accessible from the upstairs living and bedroom area. The veranda will be as large as the two downstairs bedrooms below it.

It will be perfect!

Maria offered to pay her neighbor to clean and trim the trees in her backyard. She also asked if he could do the same with her olive grove, which was located next to a dry riverbed about a ten-minute walk from her house.

In response, the neighbor offered to maintain both areas in exchange for being allowed to keep the olives he collected as payment. He would only charge her for large cleanups and supplies as needed.

Maria didn't consume much olive oil anyway and she could always pick a few olives early in the season, while they were still green, to make "tsakistes," a recipe her godmother had taught her.

To make tsakistes, she crushed the olives with a stone and then soaked them in water for a few days. After that, thick salt, garlic, lemon, and coriander seed were added.

The architectural plans for the village house were completed and approved, and the project was set to begin in the upcoming winter after Maria returned from her holiday trip.

Since the apartment was finished and listed for sale along with the garage that came with it, Maria was emptying the garage, taking the items to the village house, so that if there was an offer, the buyer could move right in without any delay.

The items were mainly inventory from her old shop, and mostly included antique pieces, souvenirs, DVDs, and many books.

Maria was delighted with her collection of movies, books, and vintage items that she had accumulated over the years.

The Greek souvenirs, magnets, small pottery, postcards, and travel guides would make excellent gifts for years to come, and Maria could also even sell some of them online in the future.

The rest she would use to decorate the village house.

The upstairs, where she would reside, would be bright and cheerful, while the downstairs would have a more conventional appearance.

And, as she had offered movie rentals and a book exchange service at the shop, she had collected ample good movies and books which she will place on built-in shelves downstairs to share with her guests.

HER PLANS TO MOVE TO a small village in the Arcadia area were met with criticism, even from her own mother.

People would ask her what she would do there and why she wanted to live in a small village.

However, Maria had always gone against the tide and was used to such criticism.

She believed that if you want something, you should work towards it and not let fear stop you.

Only dead fish go with the flow.

She believed that her children would want to come and stay in the village someday, as many wineries were opening up in the area and her children often visited *Temecula Wineries* in Southern California for weekend getaways, birthdays, and weddings of their friends.

Additionally, the village was less than a half-hour drive to the port, and Maria was sure that more cruises and water transportation would soon be offered.

It was already happening.

Maria recalled the movie *Under the Tuscan Sun* that she had watched a few years ago and thoroughly enjoyed.

She had watched it multiple times because it resonated with her.

In the movie, there was a memorable conversation between Frances (the main character) and Martini (the mayor):

Frances: "I don't want to be blind anymore. … I wake up in the middle of the night, thinking, 'You idiot, you're the stupidest woman in the world. You bought a house for a life you don't even have.'"

Martini: "Then why did you do it?"

Frances: "Because I'm sick of being afraid all the time and because I still want things."

Martini: "Between Austria and Italy, there is a section of the Alps called the Semmering. It is an impossibly steep, very high part of the mountains. They built a train track over these Alps in order to connect Vienna and Venice. They built these tracks even before there was a train in existence that could make the trip. They built it because they knew some day, the train would come."

Yes, the train will come. Maria believed that things would work out for her also.

Her friends and her children will visit her and maybe even spend more time with her as they grow and mature and have their own families.

As far as Maria was concerned, the downstairs part of the house already belonged to her children, and she was planning to give them a key once the renovation was completed.

She had decided to buy a property in her maternal family village, Aetohori, instead of her paternal family mountain village of Kastri where she was born, because the climate of her maternal village was dry, similar to that of the Eva area.

Winters in Kastri were cold and difficult with heavy snowfall. Moreover, she felt a strange energy in Kastri that made her feel a bit depressed, possibly due to suppressed memories.

The dry hot and sunny climate had been the reason she bought a house in the Palm Desert area. However, soon after she bought it, she had to rent it out and move to Greece.

FOR HER UPCOMING VISIT, Maria decided to book a stay at a spa resort instead of renting a condo and car, mostly due to continuing inflation.

She had previously celebrated her birthday with her kids at this resort, which had a traditional Italian restaurant and mineral water filled swimming pools and jacuzzies.

Maria had found that the mineral water made her skin soft and hydrated for a few days, and her daughter had noticed it also.

As she planned to stay there for a month and a half, she decided to book a mini suite for her kids and friends to be able to visit and possibly stay over comfortably.

Maria planned to rent a car and drive out for Thanksgiving and Christmas celebrations, unless the kids preferred to spend them at the resort.

She got online and saw that the resort restaurant was offering holiday meals. *Even better. Simplicity, the ultimate sophistication.*

By now Maria had become more focused.

She had stopped wasting her time and energy on small and unimportant details, and people who didn't matter.

Also, she had learned how the local village system worked and acted accordingly, just like she did with her audit assignments.

She smiled but kept her distance from gossip and drama discussions.

Maria had always been clear about her life goals and capable of finding the path to achieving them.

Although attaining financial independence was taking a while, she now understood that reinventing oneself was a challenging task that required patience and persistence.

Maria rose from her desk and walked out to her balcony. The summer had been uncomfortably hot, but now it was over.

September had arrived and with it came comfortable warm and sunny days. The yellow-brown leaves of the grapevines and fig trees, that had dried up from the scorching sun, were now falling to the ground.

As she stood there, feeling the sun's warmth on her face and body, she gazed over at the ancient Nisi hill across the bay wondering what the young man she had climbed it with so many years ago was doing.

She had a feeling that he was working on important assignments that needed his attention and that he couldn't be with her now, but that he would be visiting her soon, as he had done many times before.

Because of the few homes in Aetohori and the open mountain and valley areas, at night, Maria will be able to look up and see into the vast universe—the different constellations, the Double Cluster, the Milky Way, the many stars, and all the activity up there that she often wondered so much about.

And of course, she will witness first-hand the yearly beloved Perseid meteor shower!

Need to get a stronger telescope to see more. Need to look into that.

A couple of years before, Maria had bought a telescope for viewing far distances, but lately, she noticed that many ordinary people were posting amazing pictures of all sorts of universal phenomena.

As she turned off the lights and got ready to sleep, she had visions of sitting out on her large village house patio, with friends and family, on a hot August night, chatting into the early morning hours, while looking up into the heavens as stars rained down and all around.

Reminiscing about her life, Maria sang herself to sleep that night.

"*Oh, I've seen fire and I've seen rain, seen sunny days that I thought would never end, seen lonely times when I could not find a friend,*" then, as a single tear ran down the side of her face, she took a deep breath and continued, "*but I always thought I'd see you again … one more time again …*"

EPILOGUE

In *The Iliad*, Homer explained how the god Hephaistos gave origin to Achilles' shield while describing the *"constellations that crown the heavens, Pleiades and Hyades, the mighty Orion and the Bear, which men also call by the name of Wain."*

At ancient times most constellations were simply known as the objects or animals they represented, however, over time, most of them came to be associated with myths, to the point that, (according to writer Jean Seznec), *"stars were no longer merely identified with certain gods or heroes, but actually were perceived as divine."*

Some believed the Antikythera Mechanism was used to chart the stars.

During the second century BC, the Greco-Roman astronomer Ptolemy of Alexandria grouped *"1,022 stars into 48 constellations."* And although his astronomical chart did not include the constellations seen from the southern hemisphere, it did form the basis for the current chart of 88 constellations officially designated by the International Astronomical Union.

THE NAMES OF THE STARS WERE influenced by both Greek and Roman cultures, but the myths behind the constellations have their roots in ancient Greek mythology. And the names of constellations and planets also come from Greek and Roman mythology, with each planet bearing a name according to its unique characteristics:

- *The planet which revolves fastest around the sun was given the name Mercury, after the speedy "messenger" god.*
- *The goddess of love and beauty, Venus, is the planet which shines the brightest.*
- *Mars, the god of war, gave his name to the planet which is as red as blood.*
- *Jupiter, named after the most important Roman god, is the largest planet in our solar system.*
- *The moons in our system have also been given the names of mythological figures. The four moons of Jupiter are called Io, Europa, Ganymede, and Calisto, for the four goddesses who were desired by, and abducted by, Jupiter.*

Entire constellations were named after myths as well, allowing each one of us a fascinating glimpse back in time to when they were named.

IN 1992 WHEN THE COMET passed near the Earth, the Perseids were far more intense than their usual 60 meteors per hour. Instead, the passing of the comet produced brief bursts of up to several hundred per hour, many of which were dazzlingly bright and spectacular.

AT LEAST TWO METEOR RESEARCHERS predict that in 2028, a meteor storm will occur, and the Perseids will provide an even more spectacular show.

This will happen when "the Earth passes within 37,000 miles of a stream of debris that Swift-Tuttle released into space back in 1479."

Meteor researcher, Mikhail Maslov from Russia, also expects that a meteor storm will occur in 2028. His calculations suggest a meteor shower of perhaps 250 to 300 meteors per hour.

Esko Lyytinen, a well-known Finnish meteor expert, calculated that in 2028 the Perseid meteor shower could produce up to 1,000 or more meteors per hour.

"Under the Stars"

by John Legend

Here we are, under the stars
Here we are, under the stars
Heaven is not so far
Under the stars

We'll find a love to hold our hand through the cold
We'll find an angel light out in the storm
We'll see a light to lead us all the way home
And wherever we go we will know
Here we are, under the stars

Let's raise a toast to all the good days to come
Let's celebrate the seas that come out as one
Let's save a kiss for us and the night is done
Oh my love I'll keep you warm
Here we are, under the stars

Here we are, under the stars
Heaven is not so far
Heaven is not so far
Under the Stars

Book 1 of the *Artemis Child Peloponnese Series* was published in October 2022.

It's about Greek-born Maria who grew up in the United States and was living in Southern California until a breakdown brings her back to Greece, to her birthplace in the east coast of the Peloponnese where she is working on healing and rebuilding herself.

After surviving the difficult transition and adjusting to her new environment, Maria realizes that her life experiences and her personal legend had not only guided her back to her roots, for they also brought her back to her destiny—to solve ancient mysteries of the Peloponnese.

Along with Maria's action-filled life changing transition, it includes some of the difficulties encountered by a foreigner trying to fit in a small traditional port town on the east coast of the Peloponnese.

The book also includes a recount of ancient history—the cause of the Trojan War—along with research, findings, and analysis on some of the mysteries of ancient Argos and ancient Mycenae. It also includes research and findings of some ancient Arcadian towns and districts—such as Thyrea, Anthini, Cynuria, Tegea, Caryatae, and Sparta.

The author has also published a one-hundred-page matching companion Peloponnese travel notebook journal for those interested in visiting places mentioned in the book and taking notes.

You are welcome to visit and join her on
The Peloponnese Experience Facebook group site.

ABOUT THE AUTHOR

Diane Ioannou was born in a small mountain village on the Parnon Range of the Peloponnese. She is one of five children. When she was four years old her family moved to Chicago for a chance at a better life. She grew up in Chicago, but she would not live her life out there. That's because she found her traditional home life overbearing and even oppressive.

After her parents had started pressing her to get married, at the age of eighteen, Diane moved to Southern California. There she lived with relatives while going to college. She worked at their chain of restaurants while also working toward a higher education.

Diane would go on to earn a bachelor's degree in accounting and pass the exams to become a CPA.

After graduating she would meet her husband and soon marry and have a family. However, the marriage did not work out. She would go through a divorce while her children were still quite young.

While raising her two children she worked full-time as an auditor and tax preparer. As they got a bit older, she took evening classes for a master's degree in taxation.

Not long after her eldest started university, just as she thought life would get easier, she went through another life transition. A breakdown that brought her back to Greece, to a small port town not far from her place of birth.

The author is now working on a series of books on Peloponnese's antiquity which she finds to be full of uncovered mysteries. Diane named the series ARTEMIS CHILD. A title that represents the type of strength and endurance she found inside herself. For in her last most difficult transition, Diane found that "bravery unlocks truths." And she shares these truths with her readers.

In each book, the author also includes some of her personal experiences. Her adventures and trials and trib-ulations. Living in Greece and the difficulties in adjusting to a new environment. Including local culture and related unexplained happenings.

And lastly, the author shares her research and findings of unsolved ancient mysteries with recounts of related history and mythology. Of the very ancient "Mythical Peloponnese."

Author's Note

I f you enjoyed the novel and are comfortable doing so, please leave a review on Amazon and/or Goodreads.

Thank you!"

Facebook Diane Ioannou author page:
https://m.facebook.com/profile.
php?id=100085783783023

Facebook group:
"The Peloponnese Experience":
https://m.facebook.com/
groups/733121187755230?group_
view_referrer=search